THE ENVIRONS OF ST. PETERSBURG
PETRODVORETS-LOMONOSOV
PUSHKIN-PAVLOVSK

BONECHI
WB

© Copyright 1995
WELCOME BOOKS
Fadeeva 1,
125047, Moscow, Russia
Telex 411238
Fax 095-2509342

© Copyright 1995
CASA EDITTRICE BONECHI
Via Cairoli 18/b
50131 Firenze, Italia
Telex 571323 CEB
Fax +55-5000766

* * *

ISBN 88-8029-258-7

Text by: *Pavel Kann*
Designer: *Alexander Voeykov*
Translated by: *Michail Nikolskiy*
The photographs: *Juriy Bykovskiy, Evgeniy and Danyil German,*
Vladimir Melnikov and from photograph collections of Fotokhronika *TASS* and *APN*

INTRODUCTION

The beautiful places in the environs of St. Petersburg which lie in a semicircle, not unlike a necklace, to the south of the former capital of Russia are famous all over the world. The palace-and-park ensembles of Petrodvorets (formerly Peterhof), Lomonosov (formerly Oranienbaum, which has been given the name of the great Russian scientist of encyclopedic knowledge), Pushkin (formerly Tsarskoye Selo, renamed in honour of the great Russian poet), and Pavlovsk (out-of-town residence of Emperor Paul I) are outstanding achievements not only of Russian, but also of world culture. All major stages of the development of palace-and-park art are embodied in the ensembles that are to be seen in the environs of St. Petersburg: the parks are noted for their collections of fine specimens of marble and bronze sculpture by classical, Russian and West European masters, and the palaces are not only remarkable masterpieces of 18th and 19th century architecture, but also depositories of superb collections of painting, sculpture and decorative and applied art.

The parks created in the first half of the 18th century are distinguished by a symmetrical layout with straight alleys bordered by carefully mowed lawns and trees with decoratively cut crowns and by extensive use of geometrical motifs in the patterns of parterres. This "regularity" is particularly characteristic of the parks in the environs of St. Petersburg dating from the first half and mid-18th century. (At the time, the baroque style was prevalent in the architecture of the Russian capital.)

Thus, the Great Palace in Peterhof and the Catherine Palace in Tsarskoye Selo, built to the designs of Francesco Bartolomeo Rastrelli, were surrounded by green tracts of regular gardens and parks. During this heyday of Russian park-and-garden art the architecture of minor forms developed by

leaps and bounds: summerhouses, pavilions and bridges built at the time were true masterpieces of architecture and decorative art. These structures were given no less serious attention than major edifices and their designs embodied a lot of wit, fantasy and taste. Not only the artistic appearance of these structures, but also their location in the overall ensemble of a park acquired great significance. Skilful positioning of summerhouses and pavilions and a happy choice of architectural forms helped achieve harmony between art and nature.

In the second half of the 18th century the splendid and graceful baroque style in architecture exhausted its potentials. Following its acme, it rather soon went out of fashion, having given up its place to classicism — adherence to the traditions of classical architecture with its precisely balanced composition, laconic architectural forms and relatively modest (as compared with the baroque) sculptural décor of buildings.

During that period, in the field of park architecture a departure from the decorative character of regular parks was observed and various landscapes that were close to virginal nature and seemed to have naturally developed began to be created.

The period of transition from the baroque to classicism (early classicism) is embodied in such works by Antonio Rinaldi as the Toboggan Hill pavilion and the Chinese Palace in Oranienbaum. Classicist trends are more evident in the design of the Gatchina Palace (1766-1781), characteristic of which is graceful simplicity rather than magnificent richness.

A vivid embodiment of the ideas of landscape architecture is to be seen in Pavlovsk. The palace-and-park ensemble of this suburb of St. Petersburg was created by Charles Cameron, Vincenzo Brenna, Giacomo Quarenghi, Andrei Voronikhin, Carlo Rossi, Pietro Gonzago, and several other great masters of palace-and-park architecture.

In the years of the Hitlerite invasion the Nazis, having occupied Peterhof, Pushkin and Pavlovsk, brutally destroyed everything that could not be plundered. The suburban palaces were reduced to heaps of charred ruins. After World War II these masterpieces were raised from the ashes. It will not be an overstatement to say that the restoration of the palace-and-park surroundings of St. Petersburg was as great an exploit as the creation of these superb ensembles.

Naturally, not all the environs of St. Petersburg boast such outstanding artistic values. The out-of-town royal residences were situated to the south of St. Petersburg, whereas to its north, on the Karelian Isthmus, there were no artistic attractions of such great significance.

In the settlement of Kuokkala (now Repino), a highly revered monument of Russian culture, the Penaty museum estate where Ilya Repin, the great Russian artist, spent the last thirty years of his life, is carefully preserved.

In this resort area in the environs of St. Petersburg there are quite a few scenic spots and sandy beaches. Forest tracts protect this area from cold northerly winds and the westerly sea wind makes the climate more temperate and humid: that is why winters are moderate and summers are not hot here.

A. Martynov. Tsarskoye Selo. View at the Catherine Palace. Lithograph. 18th c.

PETRODVORETS

The old, original name of this suburb, Peterhof, which means in German "Peter's Court", is still in use today, successfully resisting its new, artificial name, Petrodvorets, given to it in 1944. Petrodvorets lies on the southern shore of the Gulf of Finland 29 kilometres from St. Petersburg.

The history of Petrodvorets goes back to the early 18th century, when it was built as a monument to the victories won by Russia in the struggle to find an outlet to the Baltic Sea. Almost all its ornamentation is permeated with the idea of glorifying the country's naval might. The southern shores of the Gulf of Finland were from ancient times inhabited by Russians and from the 12th century they were part of the lands of the boyar republic, Great Novgorod. The territory of the feudal Novgorodian republic was truly vast: it was four times as large as the area covered by France today. In 1478, the bell that used to call the people of Novgorod to a "veche" (citizens' assembly) became silent, for the Novgorod lands were incorporated in the Grand Princedom of Muscovy. In 1617, Sweden seized from Russia the southern shores of the Gulf of Finland and all the lands lying between the rivers Narva and Volkhov. Russia found herself cut off from the Baltic Sea. Her political, economic and cultural ties with the European countries were thus broken.

A clever and far-sighted politician, Tsar Peter the Great was aware that Russia could not develop without access to the sea. The Sweden of the period, however, was one of the strongest states in Western Europe: at the time, the territories of present-day Sweden, Norway and Finland and some of the lands on the southern coast of the Baltic Sea were under the power of the Swedish crown. The war waged by Russia for the restitution of what were from time immemorial Russian lands and for her establishment on the Baltic, which has become known in history as the Northern War (1700-1721), was bitter and gory. During the Northern War, in 1703, the fort and sea port of St. Petersburg, which was to become later in 1712 the capital of Russia, was founded. Russia's victory in the Northern War restored her access to the Baltic Sea.

In order to protect the sea approaches to St. Petersburg the fortress of Kronschlot was built on the sandbank near the island of Kotlin. Later on, a fortress was built on the island itself. It was given the name of Kronstadt. Peter frequently visited Kotlin and so on the southern shore of the Gulf of Finland a small rest house, the Peterhof, was built for the tsar. This house was situated slightly to the west of the present centre of the Petro-dvorets ensemble.

While the Northern War was still in progress, Peter the Great showed little concern for the ornamentation of these places, but after the victory at Poltava (1709) and the naval victories at Gangut (Hanko) and Grengam (1714 and 1720) he decided to build near his new capital a city-monument which would immortalize Russia's victory over Sweden. Besides, Tsar Peter wanted his favourite brainchild, Peterhof, with all its splendour to bear witness to Russia's wealth and glory. During his trip to France, Peter admired the royal palace at Versailles. The parks and palaces built for the king and his retinue cost France a sum equal to an annual income of the country's population. The Russian tsar became infatuated with the idea of having a "garden (that is, a park) better than the French king has at Versailles".

The land on the southern shores of the Gulf of Finland was largely marsh and clay, and so considerable irrigation work had to be carried out before the gardens and parks of the new city-monument could be laid. The thick clay was removed in layers and replaced with soil and fertilizer brought up on barges. On the orders of Tsar Peter, tens of thousands of maples, limes, chest-nuts, fruit trees and shrubs were brought to Peterhof from other parts of Russia and from European countries. The new plantations were frequently destroyed by floods and storms, but

the replanting went on again and again... Ships brought to Peterhof fine statues and paintings, rich fabrics, building materials, and parts for the construction of fountains.

Once the Northern War was over Peter accelerated the construction of Peterhof. He personally took part in designing the plans, not only providing general directions for the builders, but frequently detailing particular tasks and showing precisely how they should be carried out. In particular, he thought out the subjects of the fountain groups and, in laying out the alleys, he took care to ensure that all the garden ornaments, fountains and pavilions should be seen from various points of view.

A major part in building the unique estate of Peterhof was played by a number of gifted Russian and foreign architects and sculptors such as Johann Friedrich Braunstein, Mikhail Zemtsov, Francesco Bartolomeo Rastrelli, Niccolo Michetti, Mikhail Kozlovski, and others.

The Peterhof palace-and-park complex comprises seven parks with a combined area of more than 800 hectares, over 20 palaces and pavilions and a huge number of fountains.

During the Second World War the Nazis destroyed everything that could be destroyed and plundered everything that could be plundered. On January 19, 1944, when Peterhof was liberated, it presented a terrible picture of desolation. Only charred ruins remained of the beautiful palaces and the lovely parks were marred with dugouts and trenches. The Nazis had cut down 14,000 trees that were centuries old, destroyed nearly all the fountains and ducts, carried off the gilded statues of the Great Cascade, including the world-famous sculptural group showing the biblical hero Samson wrenching open the jaws of a lion with his hands...

Restoration work at Petrodvorets (thus Peterhof was officially renamed on January 27, 1944) was conducted on a grand scale. The treasures of the Peterhof palaces were returned from evacuation, statues were dug out of their underground burial places and restored and the interiors of the palaces were restored in accordance with photographs and drawings that had survived. On August 25, 1946, after a break of five years, the restored fountains of Petrodvorets were ceremonially switched on. Today the fountains of Petrodvorets rank first in the world in water discharge, the variety of shapes and the length of operation.

At the entrance to Petrodvorets to the left of its main thoroughfare, you may see the magnificent **Sts Peter-and-Paul Cathedral**, built between 1894 and 1905 to the design of Nikolai Sultanov. This cathedral, made of red brick, was built by the architect according to the traditions of Moscow stone church architecture. Pyramidal in shape, it is crowned with five tent-like steeples capped with gilded onion-shaped cupolas. The cathedral was designed by Sultanov not only to serve as a place of worship but to be used also as a kind of an observation platform, for its upper windows offer a magnificent panorama of St. Petersburg, the fortress of Kronstadt and the environs of Petrodvorets within a radius of some 30 kilometres.

To the right of the cathedral is a square closed on the northern side by a balustrade. Beyond this a green slope drops sharply down to a plateau which stretches right to the shore of the Gulf of Finland. It is the Lower Park of Petrodvorets.

Sts Peter-and-Paul Cathedral.
Architect N. Sultanov. 1894-1905.
Detail of the Cathedral.

GREAT CASCADE

The immense marble balcony at the centre of the façade of the Great Palace facing the sea commands a splendid view of the Great Cascade. It is the focus of the triumph of the fountain jets and unrestrained jubilation of the water element. The Great Cascade consists of 17 high waterfall steps, linked by five arches, 39 gilded bronze statues, 29 bas-reliefs, and 142 water jets shooting out from 64 waterspouts. The merry noise of flowing water is constantly heard over the cascade.

Falling down the broad steps lined with gilded bas-reliefs, the water flows on to the lower terraces. Here stand the figures of

Panorama of the Great Cascade.
Left: Samson Fountain.
Right: Sculpture of Actaeon. Sculptor I. Martos. 1801.

an old man with an oar and a young woman, personifying the Russian rivers Volkhov and Neva. In the first quarter of the 18th century they were connected by a canal near Lake Ladoga, thus linking Central Russia with seaways. At the foot of the cascade the water flows out through the mouths of a number of dolphins into a reservoir in the centre of which on a pedestal stands the tall *figure of Samson* wrenching open the jaws of a lion. From the lion's gaping jaws a twenty-metre jet of water spurts into the air. This fountain symbolizes Russia's victory over Sweden in the Northern War.

Around the feet of Samson jets of water spurt out from the mouths of eight dolphins, forming a wreath surrounding the hero. In recesses on the four sides of the pedestal are the heads of four lions, from the jaws of which also stream fountains.

From the upper grotto under the balustrade *Tritons*, sea gods (in Greek mythology, sons of Poseidon, god of the sea, half-men and half-fishes), blow trumpet-fountains of conch shells in honour of Samson's victory.

On August 25, 1946, when the restored fountains were ceremonially switched on, the gilded figure of Samson, which had been carried off by the Nazis, was not to be seen at the foot of the Great Cascade. A vase with a bouquet of flowers was standing in its place on the pedestal... The making of a new statue of Samson took quite a lot of time. It presented unforeseen problems, for although there were thousands of photographs of the prewar statue of Samson made both by professionals and by amateurs, no scientific photographic measurements — photographing the statue from a number of equally distant points — have been made. Sculptor Vladimir Simonov, however, re-created the statue of Samson. On September 14, 1947, the greatest jet of the main fountain complex of Petrodvorets spurt into the air.

On the central terrace of the Great Cascade stands the original *Basket fountain* which consists of 28 crisscrossed jets around the edge of a huge basin and 11 vertical columns of water which rise from the centre in imitation of a bouquet of flowers. In the allegorical language of the 18th century a basket of flowers or fruit signified wealth and abundance.

On opposite sides of one of the lower terraces you can see the figures of two gladiators facing each other. They hold in their hands extinct torches and wriggling snakes symbolizing victory in war and conquest over the enemy. From the mouths of the snakes water spurts in strong jets. Behind the gladiators are the figures of frogs that seem to be teasing each other with jets of water. These frogs, symbolizing the rulers of Sweden, are also an allegory subordinated to the general idea of the Great Cascade.

The gleaming golden *statue of Perseus* standing on the Great Cascade is a symbolic representation of Peter the Great himself (it should be noted that Perseus holds in his hand the cut-off head of Medusa which, in fact, is a likeness of Charles XII of Sweden).

Still another allegorical figure is the *statue of Actaeon*, a beautiful youth with antlers growing on his head. One of the myths of ancient Greece has it that Actaeon dared to watch Artemis, the goddess of hunting (identified with the Roman goddess Diana), bathe. The angry goddess changed Actaeon into a stag, and he was torn to pieces by his own dogs.

From the eastern wing of the Great Palace a broad straight road leads to the **Alexandria Park**. In the reign of Peter the Great this area belonged to Alexander Menshikov, the tsar's closest retainer, and in the 1730s it was used as a menagerie. Later on, Nicholas I presented this park to his wife, Alexandra, after whom the park was given its name that has survived to this day. Of particular interest in this park is the *Court Chapel*, built in 1831-1833 by the architects Adam Menelaws and Joseph Charlemagne to a drawing by the Berlin architect Karl Schinkel, and the *Cottage Palace*, built by Adam Menelaws in 1829. In the mid-19th century the building of the palace was altered by the architect Andrei Stakenschneider. It was not infrequently used by the royal family as a summer residence.

On the right side of the road leading to the Alexandria Park are the graceful *Ladies-in-Waiting Houses* built in 1850 in the rococo style by the architect Nikolai Benois, the head of the famous family that contributed greatly to the development of Russian culture and art. Here you can see a highly interesting display devoted to the talented Benois family which has been set up with the participation of quite a few members of the family now living abroad.

Here Actaeon is an allegorical representation of Charles XII of Sweden who has been punished for his impudence and is now trying to escape from pursuit by his former allies in the Northern War, who have gone over to the side of Russia.

The subjects of the other sculptures of the Great Cascade also have an allegorical meaning. The Great Cascade itself is the compositional centre of the whole architectural and artistic complex at Petrodvorets. The Great Cascade took its initial shape back in the Petrine days, but it was only in the mid-19th century that it acquired its present-day appearance.

The plumbing for the Petrodvorets fountains, the greatest in the world, was built in 1721-1722 under the supervision of Russia's first hydraulics engineer, Vassili Tuvolkov. The intricate water supply system stretches for some 22 kilometres, from the Ropshino Heights to Peterhof. The water flows into the fountains through the ducts and piping under its own pressure. To this end, use is made of the natural features of the area sloping gently towards the sea. There are no pumping plants here and the fountains operate in accordance with the principle of communicating vessels. From them, the water flows into the Gulf of Finland. The Peterhof fountains were a masterpiece of 18th-century fountain-building. They surpassed the famous Versailles fountains in beauty, might, grandeur and technically rational design.

GREAT PALACE

Architecturally speaking, the Great Palace is the focal point of Peterhof. It rises 16 metres above the Lower Park and its façade is 250 metres long. The roof of the palace has an exquisite outline characteristic of the baroque style. Its central building is decorated with a gilded vase and its side wings, with cupolas. Its western wing, known as a *Wing Under Arms*, is topped with a three-headed eagle (it looks from various points of view like a double-headed eagle, which was the emblem of Russia from the late 15th century up to 1917). Above the eastern building, a *Church Wing*, rises a gilded cross.

Great Palace. Architects J. Braunstein,
J.-B. Leblond, N. Michetti. 1714-1724.
Southern Façade.
Detail of the façade.

The central, three-storied part of the palace is connected by arcaded galleries with the "Wing Under Arms" and the "Church Wing". The festive-looking exterior of the palace is embellished with rich sculptural décor. Quite noteworthy are the openwork wrought iron grilles of the balconies whose metal lace incorporates gilded monograms of Peter the Great and his daughter, Elizabeth Petrovna.

Great Palace.
Building "Wing Under Arms". 1747-1751.
Domed section of the building.

The original Great Palace (which was called "Upper Chambers" at the time) was built between 1714 and 1724 with Johann Friedrich Braunstein, Jean-Baptiste Leblond and Niccolo Michetti taking an active part in its construction. In the early 1730s, Mikhail Zemtsov participated in the construction work. In the mid-1740s, the most significant decade, the reconstruction of the building under the supervision of Francesco Bartolomeo Rastrelli, began in the history of the Great Palace.

Rastrelli maintained the original division of the palace into a central part and galleries running out to side buildings, but he added side wings which stretched south in the direction of the Upper Park. He pulled down the small wings which closed off the galleries and built in their place the "Wing Under Arms" and the "Church Wing". Rastrelli successfully combined the motifs of Old Russian architecture with characteristic baroque forms. After Rastrelli work was carried out on the palace by Jean-Baptiste Vallin de la Mothe (the Chinese Rooms) and Yuri Felten (the Dining Hall, the Chesma Room, the Throne Room, the Partridge Room). Further interior alterations were made between 1845 and 1850 by the court architect, Andrei Stakenschneider, Nicholas I's favourite.

At the next pages:

Great Palace. Main Staircase.
Right: Sculpture of Flora.

GREAT PALACE: INTERIOR

The museum displays at the Great Palace open with an exhibition showing the history of its construction.

From the exhibition room you enter *Peter the Great's Oak Study*, which presents a palatial interior characteristic of the first quarter of the 18th century. The main ornamentation here are the carved oak panels, which are the work of the talented French sculptor and carver, Nicolas Pineau. The variety of themes on these panels is worth noting, including as it does oak shields with representations of military and naval equipment, musical instruments and bas-relief portraits of Peter the Great and his wife Catherine I. Many of the oak panels in this room were destroyed during the Nazi occupation of Peterhof. Work on restoring the lost masterpieces took quite an effort, for a single oak panel took a highly skilled carver on average 18 months to reproduce. Today it is almost impossible to distinguish the panels that have been reproduced by Soviet masters from those made in the early 18th century.

This room also contains original banners that witnessed the battles of the Northern War, including the standard of Charles XII of Sweden, as well as Peter the Great's travelling clock which was made in Augsburg (Bavaria) in the early 18th century.

The next room along is the *Royal Bedchamber*. It is dominated by a carved gilded four-poster bed, made in Germany in the late 17th century. The walls of the Bedchamber are decorated with late 17th-century Chinese painted silk. Of interest among the other exhibits here are an 18th-century English clock, Chinese porcelain and an 18th-century German chest of drawers.

From the Bedchamber you pass into a room the interior of which was characteristic of early 18th-century Russian palaces. Of particular interest here are articles of faience from Delft in Holland, a cupboard made in Hamburg, and a number of other exhibits dating from the Petrine times, including portraits of Peter the Great, Catherine I and Peter's favourite, Prince Alexander Menshikov, which were painted during their lifetimes. The zigzag pattern of the parquet floor in this room was designed by Rastrelli.

The adjacent room is noteworthy for its rich décor such as gilded carving and magnificent parquet. This interior is characteristic of Rastrelli's work. He widely used mirrors in decorating the interiors of palatial rooms, thus achieving an interesting visual effect: a room seemed to be much larger than it actually was. Among the items of interest in this room are a suite of Dutch furniture, a bronze clock made by French masters and a Russian chandelier, all of them dating from the mid-18th century.

The next room along shows strong traces of the influence of classicism. The classicists, who regarded classical art as the ideal model to be followed, often represented their contemporaries as heroes of classical myths. Characteristic of classicism are realistically clear shapes, well-balanced composition and plastic perfection of drawing.

The aesthetic views of classicism are to be discerned in the works of applied art contained in this room. They include articles made in Russia in the second half of the 18th century — a suite of furniture, a chandelier and candelabra. On display here are also vases made in the same period at the Wedgwood pottery factory in England. Josiah Wedgwood invented a special "stone" clay from which he made pottery with neoclassical figures and ornamentation applied in relief on a tinted background. Later on the Wedgwood factory began to produce porcelain.

Great Palace. Main Staircase.

Great Palace:
Royal Bedchamber.
Peter the Great's Oak Study.
Blue Drawing Room.

Also to be seen in this room are portraits of Catherine the Great and her husband, Peter III, assassinated by Catherine's retainers, that were painted during their lifetimes.

The next room contains exhibits which are fine samples of mid-19th century Russian applied art. Here in a French cabinet there is a "coral" dining service, which is in fact a skilful imitation of coral made at a Russian porcelain factory.

The next room was called the *Cavalier Room* or the *Crimson Room*. Its second name is explained by the fact that throughout the 19th century and later, up to 1914, the walls of the room were covered with crimson fabric.

In preparing the present display the walls were upholstered in crimson silk ornamented with a stylized floral pattern, made at one of the Moscow mills after a piece of old fabric that had survived.

Of much interest here is a suite of furniture designed by the famous 18th-century English cabinetmaker, Thomas Chippendale, a mid-18th century German bureau made of walnut and decorated with inlaid work, an 18th-century French mirror,

clock and chest of drawers, and an old English grandfather clock. On show in the *Standards Room*, the next one, are full-dress portraits of Peter the Great, of his daughter, Empress Elizabeth Petrovna, and of Empress Anna Ioannovna.

Among the objects d'art in this room is a French 19th-century clock with beautifully sculpted figures depicting a theme from Homer's "Iliad". Also of interest here are early 19th-century French candelabra, a number of pieces of late 18th-century carved gilded furniture, and an early 19th-century chandelier of Russian make.

The next room is known as the *Study*. Note the late 18th-century French desk and bureau and the French candelabra made in the early 19th century. Also on display here is an Indian sandalwood casket which used to belong to Catherine the Great, as well as various articles of porcelain made in Sèvres (France) and Meissen (Germany). On the walls are portraits of Empress Elizabeth Petrovna, Catherine the Great, her grandson, Alexander I, as a young man, and Stanislaus II Augustus Poniatowski, the last Polish king.

Next to the Study is the *Dressing Room*. Of note here is a silver toilet set, which was a gift from Louis XV of France to Empress Elizabeth Petrovna. Connected to it is the *Lounge* with walls upholstered in genuine Chinese silk that is 300 years old. The silk covering on the great Turkish sofa, however, is the work of Russian serf craftsmen. Here you can also see a curious porcelain knick-knack, a very natural-looking likeness of Catherine the Great's pet dog.

From the Lounge you enter the *Partridge Chamber*, so called because the silk which covers its walls is ornamented with representations of partridges. Its western wall is covered with silk which has been preserved by pure accident from the early 19th century. The other walls are upholstered in an exact copy of this fabric, made during the postwar restoration of the Great Palace. Of particular value among the articles to be seen in the Partridge Chamber are a Russian girandole made in 1780, an English wardrobe of the same period, a mid-18th century French chest of drawers, and 18th-century Meissen porcelain.

Next to the Partridge Chamber is the *Eastern Chinese Study*, so named because it lies to the east of the central Portrait Gallery. In the past this room was covered in white Chinese satin and contained lacquered Chinese screens. The present décor of this room is the work of Soviet restorers.

Great Palace:
Detail of the Standards Room.
Study.
Lounge.
Partridge Chamber.

Great Palace:
Eastern Chinese Study.
Detail of décor of the Study.
Portrait Gallery.
White Dining Hall.

The *Grand Portrait Gallery*, the central hall of the palace, situated as it is along the axis of the building, directly overlooks the fountains of the Great Cascade. This luxuriously appointed room was often used by the tsar for giving audiences to foreign guests of honour. The walls of this room are adorned by female portraits hung close to one another. All of them are works by Pietro Rotari. The whole collection was acquired by Catherine the Great from the painter's widow and, according to her instructions, hung here on the walls of the Portrait Gallery. Today a total of 368 portraits are to be seen here. They were rescued during the evacuation of the treasures of Peterhof. The ceiling is decorated with a plafond (a restored work by Italian artist Bartolomeo Tarsia) showing the prospering of the state under the aegis of the sovereign's power under which wisdom, justice and peace reign supreme.

Passing through the *Western Chinese Study* you enter the *White Dining Hall*. Of interest here are stucco mouldings on the walls and in oval medallions on the piers between the windows. Note also the magnificent gilded crystal chandeliers of Russian workmanship. In the White Dining Hall there is a ceremonial table laid for 30 persons. The 196-piece faience dinner service was made in England in 1760 to the order of Catherine the Great.

The cream coloured pottery was highly appraised by Queen Charlotte of England and was therefore named "Queen's Service". The furniture in the White Dining Hall was made in the 19th century after 18th-century models.

The *Audienz* (or *Ladies-in-Waiting*) *Hall* connects the White Dining Hall with the vast *Throne Room*, having a floor area of 342 square metres. It is the work of the brilliant Rastrelli and was built in 1750 for official ceremonies and receptions. The throne, which was made by Russian craftsmen, is the original and first belonged to Peter the Great. Above the throne hangs a portrait of Catherine the Great on horseback, which is a very good likeness of the imperial model. Around the walls are portraits of various members of the Romanov dynasty. The hall is illuminated by twelve bronze chandeliers and bronze wall lights made in Russia in 1780.

Next along is the *Chesma Room*. It was decorated in commemoration of a naval battle between a Russian squadron and the Turkish fleet in June 1770 in the Chesma Bay in the Aegean Sea. The battle resulted in a resounding victory for the Russians. The paintings here (by the German artist Philippe Hackert) glorify Russia's victory over Turkey in the war of 1768-1774. Hackert was commissioned to paint the pictures in honour of the Battle of Chesma in 1771. On examining the sketches for the paintings, however, Count Alexei Orlov (who had commanded the Russian squadron in the battle) was critical of one canvas which depicted a ship exploding. Hackert replied that he had never seen an exploding ship, upon which Orlov decided to help Hackert and show him what a real explosion looked like. A sixty-cannon Russian frigate, the "Svyataya Varvara", was selected for the purpose. With the sanction of the Russian empress and the duke of Tuscany, seven miles off the coast of Livorno in Italy the "Svyataya Varvara" was packed with gunpowder and exploded. Hackert hastened to commit this extraordinary spectacle to canvas. Goethe noted that this was certainly the most expensive model that had ever been used for artistic reproduction.

In the Chesma Room foreign diplomats, Turkish diplomats included, usually waited for audiences with Catherine the Great, which took place in the adjoining Throne Room.

Great Palace:
Western Chinese Study.
Detail of décor of the Study.
Detail of the lacquered plafond.
Audienz Hall.

Great Palace. Throne Room.
Portrait of Catherine the Great.

UPPER PARK

Lying next to the Great Palace on its southern side is the Upper Park with its fountains. It covers an area of 15 hectares and is a wide parterre lined by trimmed limes. The park's adornments include four light summerhouses linked by covered alleys which are formed by rows of arches intertwined by climbing plants. We will begin our walk through the park from the southern end by the wrought-iron gates and the ten-metre pylons adorned with Corinthian columns.

The first of the fountains, the *Mezheumny*, which means "vague" or "indeterminate", is a round pool 30 metres in diameter. In its centre stands a dragon with spread wings surrounded by four dolphins with jets of water spurting from their mouths.

The next fountain you come across is the *Neptune*, which is the compositional centre of the Upper Park. It is ornamented with a three-tier sculptural group and is somewhat reminiscent in composition of a similarly named fountain which stands in front of the Rote Rathaus in Berlin. On the high pedestal of the fountain in the Upper Park stands the figure of Neptune, the god of the sea. In his right hand he holds a trident, the symbol of dominion over the waves, and on his head there is a crown from which his long locks flow down on to his shoulders.

On the four sides of the pedestal there are sea monsters spurting out jets of water, and the pedestal itself is richly ornamented with mascarons, bronze bas-reliefs, and leaden wreaths of seashells, flowers and oak leaves. On the platform round the pedestal stand twin figures of riders on winged sea horses, driving on dolphins. Besides these figures there are eight dolphins spurting jets of water, frisking about in the rectangular pool of the fountain.

Panorama of the Upper Park.

Upper Park. Mezheumny Fountain.

The Neptune fountain was brought to Russia from the German town of Nuremberg. To mark the end of the Thirty Years' War (1618-1648), the town council of Nuremberg decided to set up a large fountain in the town's market square. The work was completed between 1650 and 1658. The fountain composition consisted of 27 figures and ornaments. The town fathers, however, miscalculated: when the fountain was ready for installation, it was discovered that the amount of water in the local rivers was insufficient, and so the fountain group was taken apart and put in a barn for storage. In 1782 Paul, the heir to the Russian throne, visited Nuremberg in his travels through Europe. The town council were in need of money and so they offered to sell the Neptune to Paul. He agreed and paid a generous sum of 30,000 rubles for the fountain. In 1799 the Neptune assumed its present place.

This, however, was not the end of the fountain's history. In the 19th century the kaiser government of Germany entered into negotiations with Russia for the return of the Neptune to Nuremberg. The request was declined, but in 1896 the Russian government permitted German sculptors to take moulds of the Neptune fountain and in 1902 its copy was set up in Nuremberg.

During the occupation of Peterhof the Nazis dismantled the fountain and carried it off, but in 1947 it was found in Germany and in 1956 once more restored to its place in the Upper Park at Petrodvorets. On rising ground on the southern side of the Neptune's pool a granite pedestal was put up and set on it was a bronze statue of Apollo, a copy of the leaden figure originally set up here at the turn of the 19th century.

Nearby the Neptune and on a single axis with it is the *Oak fountain*. In the 18th century at the centre of the bowl stood a fountain in the form of an oak tree. The name has survived, although today the fountain has changed its appearance completely. In the centre of the round granite-faced bowl on a tuff pedestal cut in the shape of a six-pointed star stands the marble figure of Cupid putting on a mask, which is the work of the Italian sculptor G. Rossi (second half of the 19th — early 20th centuries). The sculpture was put up here in 1929. On the points of the star dolphins spray jets of water into the air.

Almost by the very walls of the palace there are two ponds whose name, the Square Ponds, is not quite accurate, since their measurements are 54 by 45 metres. In the centre of each pond is a marble statue surrounded by jets of water.

LOWER PARK

Now we will go down the ramp leading to the alleys of the Lower Park. In it, on an area of 102 hectares, are eight palaces and pavilions adorned with the play of four fountain cascades and numerous marble and bronze statues. A salient feature of the Lower Park is its symmetrical, geometrically clear layout.

On the left is the **Conservatory**, a single-storied building with a garret built in the baroque style in 1723-1724 to the design of Johann Friedrich Braunstein and Mikhail Zemtsov. During the Nazi occupation the building was burned down. In 1954 it was rebuilt according to an early 18th-century drawing that had survived. In 1990, a unique museum of waxworks, a kind of a competitor of the world-famous Madame Tussaud Museum in London, was set up here. Visitors to the museum will see an enraged Peter the Great interrogating his rebellious son, Alexei, and Prince Menshikov, Peter's retainer, overhearing the interrogation behind a half-open door; Empress Elizabeth Petrovna, Peter the Great's daughter, playing cards with her favourite, Count Shuvalov... The other inhabitants of the museum include Emperor Paul I, Generalissimo Alexander Suvorov, Charles XII of Sweden, and many other historical personages.

In front of the Conservatory lies a garden with a fountain in its centre. It depicts *Triton grappling with a sea monster*. The monster is rending Triton's body, yet the sea god, despite the pain, has wrenched open the jaws of the monster. The battle has frightened the turtles, which are scuttling away, each spouting a small fountain. In building this fountain in 1720, an allegorical meaning was attached to it: the fountain was called upon to serve as a reminder of the brilliant victory won by the Russian navy over the Swedes near the Gangut (Hanko) Peninsula in July 1714. Triton symbolized Russia and the sea monster and the turtles, Swedish warships.

Near the Conservatory is a square towards which one of the best-known Peterhof cascades, the *Dragons' Cascade*, also known as the *Chess Hill*, descends down a high slope.

The cascade is, in fact, an aquatic stairway with its steps having a pattern of black and white squares like a chessboard.

Upper Park. Neptune Fountain.

34

Lower Park. Triton Fountain.
Detail of the fountain.

On the upper ledge stand three brightly painted, formidable-looking winged bronze dragons with streams of water pouring out of their mouths on to the "chessboard" stairway of the cascade. On both sides of the cascade the marble figures of mythological personages stand on stone pedestals. Looking upwards from the bottom the figures on the left are Olympia (symbol of the city of Peloponnesus where stood the temple of Zeus and which was the site of the ancient Olympic games), Jupiter (the supreme deity in ancient Roman mythology, identified with the Greek Zeus), Flora (the goddess of flowers), and Neptune (the god of the sea in the mythology of the ancient Romans, identified with the Greek god Poseidon).

On the right side of the cascade are Pluto (the god ruling over the lower world and called Orcus by the Romans), Pomona (the goddess of autumn fecundity), Vulcan (the god of fire and of metalworking in Roman mythology, identified with the Greek god Hephaestus), Adonis (a handsome young man loved by Aphrodite, the goddess of love and beauty, who was killed by a wild boar sent by Ares, the jealous god of war), and Ceres (the goddess of agriculture and fertility). All these statues were created by Italian sculptors in the 18th century.

In the large square at the foot of the Chess Hill two similar fountains spurt their jets. Originally put up in 1739, they were called the *Roman fountains* because they resembled in their shape the fountains that stand before the Cathedral of St. Peter in Rome. In 1799 the Roman fountains were rebuilt and their wooden bases were faced in varicoloured marble. Each fountain stands on an eight-metre pedestal consisting of two different-sized cubes placed one on top of the other and surmounted with shallow marble bowls. The jets of water spurt into the air above the bowls and overflow into the figured basins of the fountains.

At the next pages:

Chess Hill Cascade.
Architect N. Michetti. 1721.

From the square several alleys run out radially. One of these, which runs northeast, leads to the *Pyramid fountain*. Here there are as many as 505 separate jets at various preset heights forming a pyramid. The water falls into a square basin and as it overflows, it forms four cascades of a waterfall which spills into a channel surrounding the whole edifice.

This fountain was originally built by the architects Mikhail Zemtsov and Niccolo Michetti, who were given detailed instructions by Peter the Great himself on the way the "water pyramid" should look.

Along another alley, the one leading from the Roman fountains square towards the sea, on an ornamental granite pedestal stands a monument to Peter the Great. Created by the famous Russian sculptor Mark Antokolsky, it was originally put up here in 1884. During the occupation the monument was plundered by the Nazis, but fortunately its model had been preserved in one of the St. Petersburg museums. From it, a cast was made and the bronze statue of Peter returned to its empty pedestal.

At this point in the Lower Park there are several amusing trick fountains such as the *Umbrella*, the *Oaklet* and the *Fir Trees*. They were put up after the death of Peter the Great after similar trick fountains built on Peter's orders in his day. During his lifetime wooden or iron benches looking like ordinary garden seats were placed not far from his favourite Monplaisir Palace. But the moment an unsuspecting visitor to Peterhof sat down on such a seat it spurt numerous jets of water and the drenched visitor ran away in a fright to the laughter of the ladies and cavaliers taking a stroll along the alleys.

Beyond the monument to Peter the Great is a small square garden, bordered on three sides by low buildings. Peter the Great liked to take walks and rest in this garden. In the centre of the garden stands the *Wheatsheaf fountain*, consisting of 25 jets of water arranged to form a sheaf of wheat stalks. The other fountains in the garden are called the *Bells*.

Detail of Chess Hill Cascade.
Umbrella Trick Fountain.
Wheatsheaf Fountain. On the background — Catherine's Wing.
Roman Fountains.

MONPLAISIR PALACE

The buildings which line the garden on three sides are those of the Monplaisir Palace, the gem of Petrodvorets. On the coastal side is the main, 67 metre long building of the Monplaisir. It is made of unplastered brick and pointed in white lime. It is believed that the German architect and sculptor Andreas Schlüter took part in designing this building. The overall conception of the Monplaisir Palace came from Peter himself. The palace took quite a long time to be built, from 1710 to 1723.

The Monplaisir Palace is small and very cozy. Even when the two-storied High Chambers (the main section of the Great Palace above the Great Cascade) were built, Peter preferred to stay at Monplaisir when visiting Peterhof. Here he received foreign guests, held parties and family celebrations.

We will begin our tour of Monplaisir with the eastern wing which is one of the two light pavilions connected to the central section of the palace on the eastern and western sides. A tall glass door leads from this wing to the 20 metre long *Eastern Gallery*.

The northern wall of the gallery is faced with oak panels with paintings by Dutch and Flemish masters of the early 18-th century built in among them. Two of these paintings, executed in a highly naturalistic style, are of particular interest. One of them, a "Male Portrait", is a painting made to look like an engraving and the other is "Still Life with Medals and Watches".

Monplaisir Garden. Psyche Bell Fountain.
Copy of the original work by A. Canova. 19th c.
Gallery of the Monplaisir Palace.

Monplaisir Palace:
Lacquered Study. Detail of the wall.
Ceremonial Hall.

From the Eastern Gallery an oak door leads into the *Lacquered Study*, the first of the rooms in the central part of the palace. All the exquisite ornamentation of the study is the work of Russian masters who carefully studied and expertly used the Chinese technique of lacquer painting. The décor in the *Ceremonial Hall*, the central hall of the Monplaisir Palace, is the same as in

the galleries, the walls being lined with oak panels and paintings worked into them, and a magnificent plafond on the domed ceiling. In Peter the Great's time balls, parties and diplomatic receptions were held here.

Adjoining the central hall on its western side is *Peter the Great's Naval Study*. The walls of the study are lined with oak panels and inlaid with tiles representing thirteen types of 18th-century warship. The door of the southern wall of the Study leads to the *Bedroom*. In it stands a four-poster bed under a low canopy, made to suit the tastes of Peter the Great.

From the Bedroom you pass through into the *Secretary's Room*, where the tsar's orderly had his quarters in Petrine times. This room is faced in ceramic tiles faced with Dutch landscape miniatures.

The Secretary's Room leads into the *Western Gallery*, which is identical to the one that runs on the eastern side of Monplaisir.

Note the small genre painting entitled *Friendly Conversation*, which hangs on the eastern wall of the gallery. Another genre scene hanging here, *Breakfast by the Barrel*, is also of interest. It is believed that one of the characters painted also has the face of Peter the Great.

Almost adjacent to the western wing of Monplaisir is **Catherine's Wing.** It was built by the architect Francesco Bartolomeo Rastrelli in the mid-18th century. Here in a wooden annex Catherine the Great lived in exile from the court while she was still the wife of Peter III.

Adjoining the northern façade of the Monplaisir Palace is a charming terrace fenced with a whitestone balustrade. On it stands a bronze statue of Neptune cast by an unknown Russian master in 1716. This statue did not stand here during the reign of Peter the Great: it was only brought to Peterhof in 1932.

To the west of this seaside terrace is the *Adam fountain*, built in 1721. The marble statue of Adam was executed by the sculptor Giovanni Bonazza in Venice to the order of Peter the Great. The composition of the fountain is organically linked with the layout of this part of the Lower Park. There are 16 jets round the pedestal of the sculpture pouring water into an octagonal basin, from the sides of which eight alleys lead off radially, connecting the fountain to the other structures in the park.

Symmetrically with the Adam fountain at a similar distance from the canal along which the waters of the Great Cascade, having calmed down, peacefully flow down to the Gulf of Finland stands the *Eve fountain*. The statue of Eve, just as that of Adam, was also done in white Carrara marble by the Venetian sculptor Giovanni Bonazza.

From the Eve foutain the alley leading in a northwesterly direction will take you to the Hermitage Pavilion. It was a typical conceit among the Russian monarchy to call this type of palace, that was built some distance away amid the woods of their country estates, a hermitage or retreat.

The **Hermitage Pavilion** is placed symmetrically opposite the Monplaisir Palace and occupies the same place in the layout of the western part of the Lower Park as Monplaisir occupies in its eastern part. The two-storied building of the Hermitage is comparatively low, reaching as little as 11 meters in height. It is rectangular in shape with the first floor being somewhat taller. The ornamentation of the Hermitage is plain but elegant with superb wrought-iron railings along the balconies on the first floor and modest pilasters on high bases with Corinthian capitals along the façade. The Hermitage was built to the design of the architect Johann Friedrich Braunstein.

As its name implies the Hermitage is situated in a secluded spot right by the sea. It is surrounded by a deep moat which was filled with water in the days of old and for which the only way across was by a drawbridge that could be pulled up thus isolating the visitors to the palace from the world outside.

The first floor hall of the Hermitage is quite big, its area being 80 square metres. Its huge windows afford a magnificent view of the sea and the alleys of the Lower Park.

To the west of the Hermitage is the ensemble of the **Château de Marly**. This palace was built at Peterhof between 1719 and 1723 by the architect Johann Friedrich Braunstein and named after the Château de Marly, one of the French kings' summer residences in the environs of Paris. The Château de Marly at Petrodvorets is an unpretentious two-storied square-shaped building. Its western and eastern façades have balconies with wrought-iron railings emblazoned with the monogram of Peter the Great. In front of the main (eastern) façade of the Marly there is a large rectangular pond, which in Peter the Great's time was full of fish. The keeper of the pond would ring a bell and the fish would swim to the surface to be fed.

Adam Fontain. Eve Fountain. Sculptor G. Bonazza.
Hermitage Pavilion. 1721-1725.
Château de Marly.1719-1723. Architect J. Braunstein.

On the western side of the château is a semicircular pond with three small stone bridges, divided into four sections. The bridges meet at a small platform from which Catherine the Great fed her goldfish. South of the rectangular Marly pond is the Marly fountain complex. Like the Dragons' Cascade (Chess Hill) in the eastern section of the Lower Park, the Marly *Golden Hill Cascade* is the focal point of the fountains in the western section of the park. The cascade was built in 1721-1723 to the design of Peter the Great and Niccolo Michetti. It acquired its present appearance in 1732, when Mikhail Zemtsov slightly raised the level of the steps and edged their verticals with gilded bronze plates. It was since then that the cascade became known as the Golden Hill. It is one of the most imposing fountain structures in Petrodvorets.

The descending sides of the cascade are faced in white marble and in between them 22 broad steps come down in a rhythmical sequence. When the fountain is switched on, these golden steps create the illusion of a solid and very high golden wall down which crystal-clear waters flow in a glasslike shroud. This is one of the most spectacular sights in Petrodvorets.

Above the top golden step of the cascade is a well-proportioned marble wall ornamented with statues — Neptune, the god of the sea, in the centre, Triton blasting his horn on the left, and Bacchus, the god of wine-growing and wine-making, holding a bunch of grapes and a wine cup in his hands, on the right. Under the low pedestals on which each of these statues stand on a marble wall there are three gilded mascarons of fabulous sea creatures, made to the drawings of Mikhail Zemtsov.

The marble statues of the Golden Hill are copies of classical sculptures and original works by early 18th century Italian masters purchased in Italy.

Down below at the Golden Hill two fountains, which are called the *Menazherny fountains* (from the French "ménager", "to economize"), spurt huge jets that look like they are being fired from cannon. The name is not without significance, for their 30 centimetre thick streams are not solid, but hollow. These fountains were built to the design of Peter the Great himself.

Near the Menazherny fountains, between them and the southern bank of the rectangular pond there are four distinctive fountains, called the *Triton Bells*.

Golden Hill Cascade and Menazherny Fountains.
Attic of the Golden Hill Cascade.

LOMONOSOV

This royal suburb is situated on the shore of the Gulf of Finland 40 kilometres from St. Petersburg.

The origin of the name "Oranienbaum" is not quite clear. Tradition has it that in the early period of the Northern War with Sweden in winning back the lands on the southern shores of the Gulf of Finland a hothouse with bitter orange trees was allegedly found on the site of the future Menshikov grange. There was a tablet saying "Oranienbaum" above each tree. Peter the Great ordered to give this name to the estate that he gave Menshikov as a present. Much later, in 1785, when Russian cities and towns were given coats of arms, Oranienbaum was granted a coat of arms showing a bitter orange tree with reddish-yellow fruits resembling oranges.

One of the latest versions of the origin of the name "Oranienbaum" is proposed in a 1990 publication which says that what this word actually means in German is not an "orange tree" (as has more than once been stated in the literature on the history of Oranienbaum), but the "tree of the House of Orange". William III, Prince of Orange, King of England, Scotland and Ireland and Stadtholder of the Netherlands, an outstanding statesman and military leader, commanded Tsar Peter the Great's admiration. And, although Peter the Great was unable to persuade the prince of Orange to join the anti-Turkish coalition in 1690, he retained respect for William III.

In 1703, Tsar Peter named a fortress built near Voronezh Oranienburg and presented it to Menshikov. When Peter's favourite was establishing his residence on the tract of land near St. Petersburg given him by the tsar he named it Oranienbaum. It was on February 23, 1948, that Oranienbaum was renamed in honour of the great Russian scientist Mikhail Lomonosov (1711-1765).

Construction work at Oranienbaum was carried on at a rather brisk pace in the 1750s. At the time, a fortress and a palace were built here for the heir to the Russian throne, the future Emperor Peter III, and the alleys of the park were laid out. After the palace coup which brought Catherine the Great, the wife of the over-thrown Emperor Peter III, to the throne the significance of Oranienbaum became even greater. Construction work was intensified (in particular, the Toboggan Hill pavilion was built then) and the decoration of the interiors using stucco moulding, artificial marble, mirrors, painted tapestries, and mosaic floors was conducted on a grand scale. In those days, painting and sculpture developed by leaps and bounds. In the parks, new alleys began to be laid.

Peter's Bridge across the Karost river.

During the invasion of the country by the Nazi armies the Chinese Palace, the Peter III Palace, the Toboggan Hill pavilion, and the parks were severely damaged by Nazi guns.

In the postwar period extensive work was carried out to restore the architectural monuments and improve the parks at Oranienbaum.

The architectural focal point of Oranienbaum — Lomonosov is the ensemble of the **Great Palace**. Its 210-metre façade designed to be viewed from the sea has a two-tier terrace and imposing stairways. Adjoining the two-storied main building of the Great Palace are single-storied wings. They end with the Church and Japanese pavilions. On the southern side the Ladies-in-Waiting and Kitchen wings adjoin the pavilions. They form the space of the Main Courtyard of the Great Palace.

Prince Menshikov, Peter the Great's favourite, was in the sovereign's good graces. His wealth enabled him to build at Oranienbaum a palace that was not inferior in size and splendour to any of the palaces built for Peter the Great himself. It was the biggest palace built in Russia during Peter's time.

The Great, or Menshikov, Palace at Oranienbaum was built by the architects G.M. Fontana and Johann Gottfried Schädel between 1710 and 1727. Later in the 18th century the palace was partially rebuilt by Mikhail Zemtsov, Pyotr Yeropkin, Francesco Bartolomeo Rastrelli, Antonio Rinaldi, and other architects.

The interior décor that the Great Palace had in Menshikov's lifetime was altered as far back as the 18th century.

In 1745, on the orders of Empress Elizabeth Petrovna, Peter the Great's daughter, her 17-year-old nephew Peter Fyodorovich, the grandson of Peter the Great and the son of the duke of Holstein, who was the heir to the Russian throne, was married to 16-year-old German princess, the future Catherine the Great. Brought up to respect German traditions, the heir to the Russian throne, the future Emperor Peter III, constantly demonstrated his adherence to the Prussian military ways.

Peter III's enthusiasm for Prussian drill was the reason for building the fortress called Peterstadt in the Upper Park of Oranienbaum. This toy fortress was built in accordance with all the principles of contemporary fortification science. Between 1758 and 1762 the Italian architect Antonio Rinaldi built a two-storied palace on the grounds of Peterstadt. Of the whole complex at Peterstadt only the Peter III Palace and the Honorary Entrance Gate have survived to this day.

The **Peter III Palace** is not large. In its shape it is reminiscent of a cube with one of the angles cut out, as it were. This fragment of the building is originally treated as the main façade of the Peter III Palace. Here in the concavity of the spatial form of the palace is the main entrance and above it, an elegant balcony with a latticework railing and two niches with statues in them on its sides.

Japanese Pavilion of the Great Palace.
View from the Lower Pond side.
Peter III Palace. Architect A. Rinaldi. 1758-1762.

The four rooms of the ground floor had no décor: they were used as the servants' living quarters and as service rooms. Leading to the first, main floor of the palace is a winding staircase. Here there are six small rooms situated along the perimeter of the building. The first of them, the *Anteroom*, played the modest part of a through room. Of interest here is the old walnut cabinet made in Germany in 1740. Displayed in the cabinet are porcelain toy soldiers made at the Meissen porcelain factory. These small figurines were Peter III's favourite toys: he liked to arrange them in the cabinet and admire their multiplied reflections.

On display in a showcase are military tunics, including Catherine the Great's guards tunic of green silk embroidered in gold. Above the showcase is an 18th-century portrait of Peter III by an unknown artist.

The next room along is the miniature *Pantry*. In it, the original décor only of the eastern wall has survived. The shelves of carved wood are incorporated in the overall pattern, forming a decorative panel stylized by Russian artist Fyodor Vlasov in accordance with the traditional forms of Chinese art. The same master decorated the other rooms (the Picture Gallery, the Study and the Bedchamber) on the first floor of the palace with lacquer paintings based on traditional motifs of Chinese painting.

The *Picture Gallery* lost its original appearance in the late 18th century when the paintings that adorned its walls were carried off to St. Petersburg. It was only in the course of postwar restoration work that researchers found in the archives a number of drawings which enabled them to reconstruct the architect's intention. In 1961-1962, the décor of the Picture Gallery was restored as close as possible to the original scheme. Not all of the paintings are equal in artistic value, yet the skilful wall-to-wall arrangement of the pictures lends the display a decorative character achieved by placing the canvases in accordance with their colour and palette.

The Picture Gallery of the Peter III Palace was often used for entertaining guests of honour to lunch or dinner. That is why a table with a dinner service made at the famous Wedgwood factory in England, which was brought to Oranienbaum in 1750, has been placed in the Picture Gallery.

The *Study* is worth noting for the ornamentation of its ceiling featuring stucco moulding. Its original décor has been partially restored and now you can see here an 18th-century English mirror (according to the inventory of 1765, it was precisely in the Study at the time). Also of interest are the specimens of

Apollo Belvedere. Marble. 18th century copy of the IV c. B.C. classical original.

Chinese porcelain and the Japanese cabinet-chest which are on display in the Study.

In the *Bedchamber*, superb stucco decoration of the ceiling, one of the finest works by Antonio Rinaldi, has survived. Note the "Rinaldi flower" incorporated in the stucco plafonds — a pattern which was subsequently more than once repeated by the architect, in particular, in the interior décor of the Toboggan Hill pavilion. On the walls of the Bedchamber fine specimens of 18th-century painted enamels made according to the traditions of Chinese art are to be seen. In this room there are also a number of articles of 18th-century furniture — a chest of drawers, a cabinet decorated with inlaid work, old chairs of French workmanship — and 18th-century Meissen porcelain.

In the small *Boudoir* your attention will be attracted by the stucco decorations of the room featuring episodes from the history of the fortress of Peterstadt which existed here at one time. The fortress with its towers, earthen ramparts and cannons on the fortress walls is depicted in fine relief. Shown next to it is the Lower Pond neighbouring on the Peter III Palace with a flotilla of battle galleys, ships and boats, and also scenes of a cavalry battle. The walls of the Boudoir are finished in mahogany and walnut. The pale blue satin which used to cover the walls in the 18th century has not survived. In this room you see a Chinese what-not with a display of exquisite works of Chinese applied art. Of particular note here is an ivory ball, a unique sample of the skill of Chinese carvers. The ball, together with the other balls, each smaller in size than the other, which are inside it, was cut out of a single piece of ivory.

The park laid on the grounds formerly occupied by the fortress is decorated with marble replicas of "Amor and Psyche" by Antonio Canova and "Cupid Drawing the Bow" by Etienne-Maurice Falconet, the author of the "Bronze Horseman", the famous monument to Peter the Great in St. Petersburg.

Near the walls of the Peter III Palace an interesting structure by Antonio Rinaldi, the stone *Honorary Gate*, which has been preserved unaltered to this day, is to be seen. The pylons of the arch of the Honorary Gate are decorated with modest-looking pilasters. The leaves of the gate are formed by intertwined wrought-iron strips joined together by rosettes. Incorporated in the upper part of the opening of the arch is a gilded copper bas-relief showing banners, weapons and armour. The arch is surmounted by an octagonal turret covered with an ornamented cupola and a tall slim spire. The weather vane on its top shows the figures "1757", the year that the gate was built.

Apollino. Bronze. Mid-19th century copy of IV c. B.C. classical original.

CHINESE PALACE

At some distance from the Peter III Palace to its west stands the so-called Chinese Palace, also built to the design of Antonio Rinaldi between 1762 and 1768. It should be noted that the palace came to be known by this name, a rather unconventional one, only in the 19th century. The outward appearance of the palace bears no resemblance of Chinese architecture. It is only in the décor of some of its interiors that traces of Chinese decorative motifs are to be seen. At one time the palace boasted large collections of works of Chinese decorative art and of Japanese porcelain. Today some of these works still adorn the Chinese Palace which is distinguished by particularly exquisite decoration of its interiors featuring highly varied stucco mouldings and patterns of the parquet. The wall panels, plafonds, over-the-door pictures and decorative paintings of the Chinese Palace rival their counterparts in quite a few of the finest palaces in Western Europe in splendour, workmanship and richness.

The decoration of the palace with painting was carried out and, in the main, completed between 1764 and 1768. Six of its rooms were ornamented with "painted tapestries" — canvases with decorative paintings. They have survived in the Golden Study and in Paul's Anteroom and Study. Most of the pictures and decorative painting in the Chinese Palace were executed by Italian masters. Two of them, Serafino-Lodovico Barozzi and Stefano Torelli, worked at Oranienbaum. Other artists, working in their homeland, created paintings on themes which were agreed upon in advance and which were determined by the purpose and overall decorative scheme of the interior. Thus it happened that a whole school of first-rate 18th-century Italian artists, masters of the Venetian Academy of Arts, whose work was the last creative upsurge of old Italian art which was nearing decline at the end of that century such as Gasparo Diziani, Francesco Zugno, Jacomo Guarana, and others came to be represented at the Chinese Palace. Pietro Rotari (1707-1762), who came to Russia in 1756, is represented at the palace by a small gallery of female portraits typical of this painter.

This palace was not intended for permanent residence of the royal persons and served as a stopping place during short visits to Oranienbaum, lasting not more than several hours, by Catherine the Great and her retinue. At the time, it was known as the Dutch Cottage. Over the 29 years of its existence under Catherine the Great she spent a total of 48 days at the palace. Besides the empress' retinue, a number of foreign monarchs such as Emperor Joseph II of Austria and Gustavus III of Sweden and, not infrequently, "gentlemen outlandish ministers" visited here together with her.

The Chinese Palace is a valuable monument of the period in the development of Russian architecture (superbly represented, in particular, by works of Francesco Bartolomeo Rastrelli) when the luxuriant, highly ornamental baroque style began giving way to austere classicism.

The building of the Chinese Palace is not very large: originally it was single-storied and the second story on the southern façade was only added in the mid-19th century. The palace stands on a low granite base and quite a few of its rooms have French windows facing the park.

The main suite of rooms opens with the *Hall of the Muses*, the interior of which ranks among the finest 18th-century Russian palatial interiors.

Chinese Palace. Great Hall.
Fragment of southern wall.

The hall, connected by six large French windows with the park outside, is lavishly decorated with painting and stucco mouldings and the ornamental design of its ceiling and walls corresponds to the patterns of its parquet floor. Thus, for example, the décor of the floor and the ceiling repeats the motif of a vase with flowers.

A similar vase, made in the form of a stucco moulding, is to be seen in the round niche above the door leading to the Blue Chamber. On the piers are representations of the Muses by the Italian painter Stefano Torelli. On the eastern wall you see Urania, the Muse of astronomy (there are stars above her head), and Calliope, the Muse of eloquence and epic poetry (she holds the "Odyssey", the "Iliad" and the "Aeneid", the poetic master-pieces of the classical world, in her hands). To the left of the door is Terpsichore, the Muse of dancing and choir singing, with a lyre in her hand. On the southern wall are Clio, the Muse of history, holding a trumpet, an attribute necessary for an-nouncing historical events and Euterpe, the Muse of music and lyric poetry.

On the western wall at the entrance to the Blue Chamber are Thalia, the Muse of comedy, with a theatrical mask in her hand, on the left and Melpomene, the Muse of tragedy, holding a crown and a sword, on the right. Shown on the piers of the northern wall are Polyhymnia, the Muse of sacred poetry, and Erato, the Muse of lyric poetry.

Above the eastern door is a representation of Apollo, the god of the sun and the supreme patron of the arts of the ancient Greeks. By the eastern wall on ornamental pedestals stand two busts made by 18th-century Italian sculptors — those of Lucre-tia (according to a Roman legend, a Roman woman who was dishonoured by the king's son and committed suicide) and Cleopatra, the queen of Egypt (1st century B.C.).

The *Blue Chamber* connects the main suite of rooms with the private chambers of Catherine the Great's son, the future Em-peror Paul I. Most elements of the original décor of the Blue Chamber have been lost. The pictures that are to be seen here were painted in 1860. One of the few elements of the original décor to have survived in the Blue Chamber is the Italian landscape above the door leading to Paul's Drawing Room by the Venetian painter Francesco Zuccarelli.

Next along is the *Great Hall*, the biggest and the most grand-looking room in the Chinese Palace. In this oval-shaped hall there are columns with gilded capitals on the sides of the two doors. Above the doors there are oval medallions with marble bas-relief portraits of Peter the Great and his daughter, Elizabeth Petrovna, by Marie-Anne Collot, a disciple of Etienne-Maurice Falconet. On the walls of the hall are paintings by the Venetian artist Stefano Torelli — "The Abduction of Ganymede" (the beautiful youth Ganymede, son of the king of Troy, one of the characters in ancient Greek mythology. By the will of the gods he was abducted by an eagle and carried off to Mount Olympus where he had to serve as the cupbearer to Zeus during feasts) and "Juno and a Genius". Through the image of Juno, queen of the gods in Roman mythology, Torelli glorified the imperial proprietress of the palace. There is a ceremonially laid table in this hall. The rich table appointments that are to be seen here vividly attest to a high level of 18th-century Russian applied art. The next room, the *Lilac Chamber*, is intimate and not official or ceremonial-looking in décor. The main theme of the painted ornamentation of this room is the theme of romance.

Chinese Palace:
Portrait Gallery.
Great Chinese Study.
Golden Study.
Paul I's Drawing Room.

The most significant interior in the Chinese Palace in terms of its artistic value is that of the *Bugled Study*. It is called thus because its walls are ornamented with bugle panels showing bouquets of flowers and exotic birds, trees and plants. All the pictures are embroidered in chenille (that is, tufted silk) on canvases covered with bugles — long tubular beads. On all the twelve panels there are a total of more than two million of such slender glass tubes.

When lighted, the bugles shine with every shade of pink, blue and lilac colours. In building the palace the floor in the Bugled Study was made from smalt — a kind of coloured glass. The art of making this material emerged long ago in the ancient Orient and later on it was lost.

The great Russian scientist Mikhail Lomonosov revived its manufacture in Russia. He invented (or discovered anew) a method of making smalt and in 1754 he founded the Ust-Ruditsk factory for making bugles, beads and smalt. It was at this factory that the smalt for the Chinese Palace was made. Unfortunately, the smalt floor has not survived: it was replaced with a wooden copy in 1819.

In the Bugled Study there are two tables faced in mosaics of more than ninety colours and shades — rare masterpieces of 18th-century Russian mosaic.

The *Lesser Chinese Study*, situated symmetrically with the Blue Chamber, connects the ceremonial interiors of the palace with the small suite of Catherine the Great's private chambers and is decorated with laid-on wood carvings featuring Chinese ornamental motifs. Parquet in this room, made of 15 woods inlaid to form a distinctive, highly intricate pattern, is one of the most beautiful in the palace. The ceiling or, rather the covering of the study is made in the form of a truncated pyramid ornamented on its corners with moulded figures of fantastic monsters somewhat reminiscent of dragons that are typical of Chinese folk art. In this room there are quite a number of remarkable works of Chinese and Japanese applied art, including lacquerware, articles of porcelain, and also pieces of furniture and enamels.

The *Great Chinese Study* is the last one in the main suite of rooms. Its décor is representative of the fantastic notions of the Orient characteristic of the 18th-century Russian nobility. On the walls of this room are inlaid wooden panels showing Chinese men and women, fantastic birds and exotic landscapes, made in imitation of Chinese pictures. In accordance with the traditions of Chinese painting, the salient feature of these pictures is the use of contour drawing and the absence of chiaroscuro. In this room quite a number of distinctive articles made by 18th- and 19th-century Chinese and Japanese master craftsmen are to be seen.

The *Chinese Bedchamber* is also reminiscent of the style of Chinese folk art. A major element of décor in this room are mirrors covering the walls, corners and ceiling: they repeatedly reflect the interior of the room, thus making it seem bigger than it actually is. It was in the second half of the 18th century that large-size mirrors began to be manufactured in Russia. The décor of this room features motifs of Chinese art. Fragments of the original décor have survived to this day.

The *Dressing Room* has substantially changed its appearance over the years of the existence of the Chinese Palace, particularly so after its alteration in the mid-19th century. At the time, the walnut wall facing was transferred from the Dressing Room to the Boudoir. Eleven portraits of court ladies painted by the French artist Jean de Sampsoy in 1757 became then, and still are, the main element of the décor of the Dressing Room.

The walls of the *Portrait Gallery* are adorned with 22 portraits by the 18th-century Italian portraitist Pietro Rotari. Unlike the portraits by Sampsoy which are in the Dressing Room, these portraits by Rotari are likenesses of girls of humble birth representing different nationalities.

The so-called *Golden Study*, adjoining the Portrait Gallery, is the last one in Catherine the Great's suite of private chambers. This room is named after its decorative scheme in which the golden colour dominates. The appointments of this room include an 18th-century writing desk and cabinet of French workmanship, and also items made by Russian craftsmen. Dating from the same period are the vases, candlesticks and other articles that are to be seen here. This room was Catherine the Great's study. The empress' small private library was transferred to the Hermitage in 1792.

The *Anteroom* was called thus in the 18th century because it was here, on the side of the southern façade, that the main entrance to the palace was located. Some of the elements of its décor such as, for example, the painting "Diana and Actaeon" on the western wall and the "Landscape with Ruins" are by an unknown 19th-century master. In the Anteroom there are oval tables, which were apparently made specially for the Chinese Palace in 1760, and also 19th-century furniture — a dining-room set of carved wood and a chiffonier inlaid with mother-of-pearl — and a clock in a case ornamented in a traditional Chinese style. Here you also see 18th-century vases made at the Meissen porcelain factory and 19th-century candelabra.

Of note in the *Wardrobe* are the walls faced with carved wooden panels. This carving both compositionally and stylistically corresponds to the decorative stucco moulding above the fireplace. The *Drawing Room* is one of the rooms which were set apart for the heir to the Russian throne. Only a few elements of its original 18th-century décor, including the stucco decoration of the ceiling and the painted plafond depicting Diana, the goddess of hunting in Roman mythology, have survived here.

In the *Damask Bedchamber*, which served as the bedroom of the heir to the Russian throne, the future Emperor Paul I, the plafond shows Urania, the Muse of astronomy, teaching a youth to reign and win victories, thus emphasizing the purpose of the room. There are a crown and a sceptre in the Muse's lap and in her hand she holds a statuette of Nike, the ancient Greek goddess of victory. Here there are also portraits of Paul I (a copy of the portrait by Stefano Torelli) and of Catherine the Great (an original work by the same master).

Next to the Damask Bedchamber is the small *Study*. Its walls are decorated with ornamental painting which goes well with Chinese marble and wooden plaques with carved figures, hieroglyphs and landscapes.

The suite of Paul's private chambers ends with the *Boudoir*. This room was altered considerably during the rebuilding of the palace in 1850.

Chinese Palace. Lesser Chinese Study.
Fragment of the blind.

At the next pages:
Chinese Palace. Hall of the Muses and Bugled Study.

TOBOGGAN HILL PAVILION

To the northwest of the Chinese Palace is the three-tier Toboggan Hill Pavilion, the surviving fragment of a palace-and-park "contrivance" built by Antonio Rinaldi between 1762 and 1774. The graceful lightness of the structure and the white-and-blue colour scheme of its décor lend it a trim and festive-looking appearance. Above the ground floor rise two main stories surrounded with balustrades running along the perimeter of the building. The central section of the building is surmounted with an elongated dome reminiscent of a bell in outline. The building is lavishly ornamented with columns, pilasters and decorative vases. This structure was at one time part of an amusement complex which has become known in the history of Oranienbaum as the Toboggan Hill. A 530-metre rolling wooden slope running through a wide and long clearing adjoined the terrace of the pavilion's southern façade. According to one of the contemporaries, "people rode in ornamented carriages on small metal wheels along cut-in tracks down the rolling slope. The height of the slope diminished little by little to become indiscernible at the end". On the sides of the slope along the whole of the clearing stone colonnades were put up and their flat roofs were ornamented with vases and sculptural pieces and used as promenades.

In the course of time the riding structures fell into disrepair and were no longer used for pleasure riding. In 1813 part of the structure collapsed. In 1858-1861 the slopes and the colonnades were pulled down and now only the elegant pavilion is to be seen at the end of the clearing as a reminder of the unique Toboggan Hill complex that existed here in the days of old.

The palace-and-park complex of Oranienbaum — Lomonosov was outside the area occupied by the Nazis during the war and was thus preserved in a much better condition that the other suburbs of St. Petersburg, which is why its sights are of particularly great historical value.

PUSHKIN

Tsarskoye Selo, a gem of Russian national culture, is a complex of unique palaces and parks built by great 18th- and 19th-century Russian and West European architects. In 1937 it was renamed in honour of Alexander Pushkin (1799-1837), the great Russian poet. Here everything — the building of the Lyceum at which he studied for six years and the shadowy walks of the Catherine Park — reminds you of Pushkin's poetry. It was here that his gift for poetry shaped up and it was here that Pushkin created his first poetic works.

In the spring of 1831, after the years of his study at the Lyceum and the period of his forced travels or, rather, exile had passed, Pushkin together with his young and beautiful wife, Natalie, settled down in Tsarskoye Selo and spent a summer here in a cottage which has survived to this day (its present address is 2 Pushkinskaya Street).

The town of Pushkin is situated 24 kilometres to the south of St. Petersburg. Its history, just as the history of Petrodvorets, goes back to the days of old when the lands on which the town lies belonged to the Novgorodian boyar republic and subsequently to the centralized Russian state and which were seized by Sweden in 1617.

During the Northern War, after the troops led by Peter the Great won back the lands lying between the Neva and the Southern shores of the Gulf of Finland, the territory on which the town of Pushkin now stands was also liberated from Swedish rule.

This locality was named "Saari mõis", meaning "grange on an elevated spot", on a Swedish map dating from that period. In Russian, it began to be called "Saarskaya myza", "Saari grange".

In 1710 Peter the Great gave the Saari grange to his wife, the future Empress Catherine I, after whom the palace which began to be built here at the time was named. Between 1718 and 1724 the architect Johann Friedrich Braunstein built a two-storied stone palace with service wings on the site of the grange.

After the gloomy period of Bironovshchina, the domination at Empress Anne Ioannovna's court of her favourite, Biron, and of other German dignitaries had passed, Elizabeth Petrovna, the daughter of Peter the Great, encouraged the development of Russian national culture at her court. During the reign of Empress Elizabeth Petrovna (1741-1761) the palace was rebuilt more than once by prominent Russian architects, including Alexei Kvasov and Savva Chevakinsky.

In 1752 Francesco Bartolomeo Rastrelli (1700-1771), one of the greatest 18th-century architects, an outstanding master of the baroque style in architecture, was commissioned to rebuild the Catherine Palace.

Catherine Palace. Detail of the Main Façade.

Openwork Gates of the Main Courtyard.
Detail.

Having acquainted himself with what had been done at Tsarskoye Selo by his predecessors, Rastrelli decided to make an organic link between the separate parts of the building. The new palace was much taller and its azure main façades, ornamented with a great number of volumns, statues and mouldings, now stretched for more than 300 metres.

Rastrelli adorned the main courtyard in front of the palace with superb openwork gilded iron gates. The semicircular square before the palace, formed by festive-looking single-storied semi-circular wings, was the site of military parades on solemn occasions and a favourite place of the nobles residing at Tsarskoye Selo, who came here to take an evening promenade and to listen to performances of a military band.

Arriving at the palace guests would first walk along the shiningly magnificent main façade. Then, entering the palace, they would ascend the main staircase and from the upper landing an endless and majestic suite of splendid palatial halls gleaming with gold opened before them. The palace was lavishly decorated not only on the inside, but also on the outside. A total of 105.242 kilo-grams of gold was used for gilding the statues and other ornaments. The gilded ornaments shined beautifully against the façade of the building.

One of the finest interiors in the palace was that of the Amber Room. Its amber décor which was the work of Andreas Schlüter (1709) originally belonged to Friedrich Wilhelm I of Prussia. In 1716 Peter the Great gave in exchange for the amber panels 248 sturdy soldiers for the Prussian king's guard as well as a lathe and a wine cup which he had made himself. Great care and protection was given to transporting the panels to St. Petersburg from where on the orders of Empress Elizabeth Petrovna soldiers carried the priceless cargo to Tsarskoye Selo in their arms. In 1755 Rastrelli installed the panels in the Amber Room.

Since there were not enough amber panels to cover the whole room he inserted a number of mirrors on the lower part of the wall and used an excellent imitation amber for the upper part. These priceless amber panels were plundered by the Nazis and have not been found to this day.

During the reign of Catherine the Great (1762-1796) substantial alterations were carried out on the palace. The gilt on the ornaments and sculptures (which at the time were wooden) had not lasted long. The empress ordered them to stop any further gilding, take down the wooden statues that were peeling, and paint the moulded ornamentation. An extra story was built on the side wings and entrances added, and the palace was given the appearance it has largely retained to this day.

To the northwest of the Great Palace the New Garden (the present Alexander Park) was laid and adjoining the garden façade of the palace on its southeastern side was the Old Garden, known today as the Catherine Park.

The second half of the 18th century is marked by the establishment of neoclassicism in Russian art and architecture. And it was in this style that between 1760 and 1790 a whole constellation of talented architects such as Charles Cameron, Giacomo Quarenghi, Vassili and Ilya Neyelov, Yuri Felten, and Antonio Rinaldi worked at Tsarskoye Selo. It was during this period that some of the finest buildings were put up here, including the Alexander Palace, the Cameron Gallery, the Concert Hall, the Upper and Lower Baths, and also the building which housed the Lyceum and a number of other structures.

In the years of the Great Patriotic War the town of Pushkin suffered great damage. Many priceless treasures perished in the flames of the fires and many works of art were brutally destroyed or plundered. Centuries-old trees were chopped down in the old parks, unique pavilions and beautiful statues were demolished by bomb and shell bursts...

After the town of Pushkin was liberated on January 24, 1944, scholars, historians and restorers began their selfless intricate work on the restoration of the palaces and parks and the re-creation of the original appearance of Tsarskoye Selo.

Palace Church.

Detail of the Fence of the Main Courtyard.

Catherine Palace:
Main Staircase.
Cavaliers' Dining Room.

CATHERINE PALACE

The Catherine Palace once again assumed its festive look created by the colour scheme of its façade with azure walls, white columns and platbands and dark-green capitals.

The *Main Staircase* built to the design of the architect Ippolit Monighetti in 1860 is in the centre of the palace and occupies the whole space between its western and eastern façades. The white marble steps and the Japanese and Chinese decorative porcelain plates and vases contribute to the magnificence of the interior. The paintings on the ceiling are the work of 17th- and 18th-century Italian artists. The composition in the centre is the "Judgement of Paris".

The first room that we enter from the Main Staircase on the way to the southern side of the palace is the *Cavaliers' Dining Room*, which was built by Rastrelli. Destroyed during the war, it was completely restored in the postwar years. This room seems to be lighted thanks to the abundance of sculptures, wreaths and shells gleaming with gilt, which are reflected and multiplied by the mirrors. In one corner is a tiled stove elegantly ornamented with niches and columns which is characteristic of Rastrelli's interiors.

The stucco ceiling is covered with a canvas by an unknown 18th-century master which depicts Helios, the sun god, riding in his chariot across the skies. The gilded chairs here are also by Rastrelli. The figured table which stands by the windows is laid with the so-called Hunter's Service, which was made at the St. Petersburg porcelain factory in 1760.

From the Cavaliers' Dining Room tall arched doors lead into the enormous (floor area, 846 square metres) *Great Hall* (also known as the *Throne Hall*) of the palace. Its décor is a brilliant specimen of the baroque style embodying Rastrelli's great talent at its best. The hall with two tiers of windows seems boundless: this effect is created through the use of mirrors inserted in the piers between the windows. The doors and the frames of the mirrors in the Throne Hall are covered with carved wreaths featuring fanciful shells, female figures and cupids shining with abundant gilt.

On the other side of the Main Staircase is the *Picture Hall*. Of the 130 canvases that hung here before the war the 114 most valuable were evacuated and for this reason have been preserved. This is one of the finest rooms in the Catherine Palace, taking up the whole width of the building. Its walls are completely covered with paintings, a substantial share of which were purchased in 1745. They are works by 17th- and early 18th-century Dutch, Flemish, French and Italian painters. Besides the genre paintings there are two interesting battle pieces on scenes from the Northern War waged by Russia against Sweden.

Catherine Palace. Great Hall.
Architect F.-B. Rastrelli. 1750.
Detail of the Hall.

Catherine Palace:
Alexander I's State Study.
Green Dining Room. Architect Ch. Cameron. 1780.

The interior of the Picture Hall is truly magnificent: it is bathed in sunlight coming in through two tiers of windows on either side, its doors ornamented with elegant representations of female heads shine with gilt, and its beautifully designed light parquet adds to the overall effect of exquisite luxury.

Quite interesting is *Alexander I's State Study* with the windows facing the park. Of note here is the magnificent marble fireplace ornamented with Ionic columns. The compositions on the walls feature ancient accoutrements. Under the vaults of the ceiling are scenes from the myth of Cupid and Psyche. In the study there are a number of authentic objects which were evacuated during the war and which are now in the places they used to be kept during the reign of their imperial owner. They include an early 19th-century bronze openwork chandelier from St. Petersburg, a vase made at the St. Petersburg porcelain factory in 1818 and depicting Alexander I's entry into St. Denis near Paris in 1814,

and clocks, candelabra and various other malachite and bronze items on the desk. The other objects in the room — the writing desk covered with a green baize tablecloth and the walnut furniture — were re-created after the war from material contained in the archives and an old watercolour of the state study. Leading off this room are the *Vaulted Communicating Room* and the *Oval Anteroom* with the walls of the same soft greenish hue.

Some of the interiors in the palace are the work of Charles Cameron. They include the *Green Dining Room*. Here classical motifs are dominant. The light-green walls are ornamented with moulded wreaths, figures and vases and there are rectangular medallions representing scenes from mythology on a pink background. This room has almost completely been restored to its prewar appearance. The white chairs upholstered in green cloth and the bronze fire irons are also designed by Charles Cameron.

Next along is the *Blue Chamber*, one of the finest rooms in the palace, which is also the work of Charles Cameron. Here he made wide use of carving, moulding, gilt, mirrors, ornamental silk, marble, and rare woods, combining them together to outstanding effect.

The parquet in this room is very picturesque. Much of the ornamentation is the original. Thus, the blue glass and crystal standard lamps with their bisque figures were made at the St. Petersburg glass works in the late 18th century. The carved gilt chairs and the bronze fire irons are also of the same date. But the silk with its printed dark-blue flowers is postwar, having been made at the Krasnaya Roza weaving mill in Moscow according to the old surviving specimens, and the plafond was re-created from Cameron's original drawing.

The *Carved Study* and the *Picture Study* are two elegant rooms in which carving, painting and moulding are artistically combined. Restored after the war, they now look exactly as they did when created by Vassili Stasov.

The next room, the *State Bedchamber*, also designed by Charles Cameron, is decorated in light-green and blue. Here there are many elegant ceramic pillars. The table inlaid with rare woods comes from Okhta near St. Petersburg.

Catherine Palace:
Main Enfilade.
Chinese Blue Chamber.
State Bedchamber. Fireplace.

The next one in the main suite of rooms is the *Chinese Blue Chamber*, which is so called because for 150 years its walls were upholstered in Chinese blue silk, painted with coloured Chinese landscapes and genre scenes. The whole décor of the room is completed by a number of pictures of Empress Elizabeth Petrovna in her youth where she is portrayed as Flora, the goddess of flowers (artist Georg Christoph Grooth) and a gouache by Semyon Shchedrin showing the Imatra Waterfall on the Vuoksi River in Finland.

The *Antechoir* is upholstered in silk on which are woven pictures of pheasants and swans. This material was made by Russian serf weavers on hand looms in the second half of the 18th century. The bright ceremonial effect of the silk gives the room an elegant, festive appearance.

Through the Antechoir you enter the choir on the first floor of the palace church. The choir, resembling a balcony, was used in the 18th century as the empress's pew during service. Down the narrow stone steps you descend into the main part of the church.

The *Church Antechamber*, a kind of a grand vestibule outside the main part of the church, was built by Vassili Stasov in 1843 to replace the old living quarters that had previously stood here.

LYCEUM

In 1789-1791, when the construction of the Cameron Gallery was being completed near the southern wing of the Catherine Palace, the architect Ilya Neyelov put up a four-storied detached building near the northeastern part of the palace. Very modest in design it contrasted with the luxuriant splendour of the palace, with which the building was connected by a monumental arch. The building was originally intended for Catherine the Great's grandsons, the sons of her son, Paul. The empress avoided using staircases. It was to rid her of the need to descend a stairway and then ascend another one that this arch, which linked the palace to the building was put up.

Entrance Hall.
Physics Room.
Great Assembly Hall.

The reign of Paul I was not long: he was soon assassinated and Alexander I, his son and the grandson of Catherine the Great, ascended the throne. On January 11, 1811, he instituted the Lyceum and gave instructions that it should take over the building. A certain amount of structural alteration was then carried out on the building by Vassili Stasov and in the autumn of that year thirty young boys were enrolled in the Lyceum.

This educational institution was intended for the children of "noble families". One of such old noble families was the Pushkin family.

The ground floor of the Lyceum building housed the service quarters and the tutors' flats. On the first floor was the dining hall and the pantry, a sick bay and a pharmacy, a small assembly hall, and the office. The second floor was taken up with the classrooms and the Great Assembly Hall, while on the third, top floor were the dormitories. The library, consisting in part of books from the private libraries of Catherine the Great and Alexander I, was in the arch.

The Lyceum's first intake consisted of young boys between the ages of eleven and fourteen. They studied within the walls of the Lyceum for six years, never leaving it even for holidays.

The entrance to the Lyceum building is in Litseisky Lane. The main staircase is illuminated by wall lamps made in the fashion of the oil lamps which used to be here in Pushkin's day. Nowadays the ground floor houses the service rooms of the museum and the first floor is used for storing the museum's stocks. The rooms on the second and third floors are kept exactly as they were in Pushkin's time.

On the second floor is an *Entrance Hall*, the windows of which look out on to the Lyceum garden. From here a door leads into the room, where the pupils used to read newspapers and magazines. The Lyceum subscribed to 8 foreign and 7 Russian publications. During the war of 1812 against Napoleon's Grande Armée, the pupils would sit here for long hours following the course of the fighting.

Through an arched entrance you pass into the *Great Assembly Hall*, the largest room in the Lyceum. The walls of the hall are painted in imitation of pink marble. The décor is enriched by paintings on one of the walls and mirrors on the piers. Here on October 19, 1811, the official opening of the Lyceum took place and on January 8, 1815, in the presence of Gavriil Derzhavin, the celebrated Russian poet, the young Pushkin read out his famous poem "Recollections at Tsarskoye Selo" as part of an examination. And here again on June 9, 1817, a leaving ceremony was held for the pupils of the first intake, who had finished their studies.

Beyond the Great Assembly Hall are the classrooms which look just as they did originally. The largest of them is the *Physics Room*. It is very light, having six windows, and its ceiling is ornamented with painting representing the signs of the zodiac. The class desks whose tops can be lifted are arranged in an amphitheatre and opposite them is the teacher's desk on a raised platform with three steps leading to it.

Lyceum. Pushkin's "Cell" No. 14 (Pushkin's dormitory).
Monument to A.S. Pushkin. Sculptor R. Bach.

84

Corner of the Catherine Park.

The third floor has also been restored on the basis of archival materials as it was during Pushkin's time. On both sides of the long corridor spanning the whole of the floor are the pupils' dormitories. They look not unlike narrow cabins and are divided by partitions which do not quite reach up to the ceiling. The partitions divide each window in half so that each "cell" (as Alexander Pushkin dubbed his bedroom) has half a window that can be opened freely.

In *"Cell" No. 14*, Pushkin's bedroom, there is little furniture: a narrow bed, a desk, a chest of drawers, and a washstand...

When you see these things, you get the impression that the young occupant has just gone out for a minute and will be back soon. In the small garden by the walls of the Lyceum is the *statue of Alexander Pushkin* by the sculptor Robert Bach. Paid for out of voluntary public subscription, it was laid in 1899 to mark the 100th anniversary of Pushkin's birth and unveiled in 1900. One of the finest monuments to Pushkin, it depicts the poet in his youth, wearing the uniform of a pupil at the Lyceum and sitting pensively on a garden seat. The poet seems lost in a world of poetic thoughts and sounds...

Next to the monument is an old church, built between 1734 and 1747 by the architect Karl Blank. It is the oldest of the structures that have survived at Tsarskoye Selo.

Opposite the Lyceum building the trees of the Catherine Park rustle their leaves. Very picturesque and quite varied are its landscapes with groves, ponds and meadows giving place to rows of broad and straight alleys and carefully trimmed shrubs. Skilfully selected species of trees, masterly use of flower beds and sculptures in decorating the park and an abundance of small clearings and bridges are in an inimitable and harmonious way combined with the palaces and pavilions to form a single spectacular whole.

UPPER BATH

To the southeast of the centre of the garden façade of the Catherine Palace is the "regular" part of the park laid in accordance with the traditions of French park architecture. Situated in this part of the park is a pavilion known as the Upper Bath. It was built by the architect Ilya Neyelov in 1777-1779 to be used as a bathhouse for the royal family. Externally the pavilion is fairly modest in appearance, but the interior was once very fine indeed. Besides the pool and the baths, there was also a rest room here, which was beautifully ornamented with decorative painting. The interior décor of the Upper Bath was based on sketches of the painted ornamentation of the Golden House of the Emperor Nero made during excavations in Rome in 1776. The plafond on the ceiling and two panels above the doors depict scenes from the myth of Phaethon, the son of Helios, the sun god. Besides the mythological scenes, there is also decorative painting here, including a representation of Venus making her toilet and garlands of flowers and fruits.

The Upper Bath has the triple-edged projection on its façade towards a pond and next to it is a path lined with marble sculptures of gods and goddesses by early 18th-century Italian sculptors. There is a statue of an Amazon holding a shield which depicts an eagle fighting with a lion. Opposite the Amazon is Hercules, as an allegorical representation of Peter the Great. One of the finest statues to be seen here is that of Galatea sitting on a dolphin by the sculptor Pietro Baratta.

CAMERON GALLERY

From the side of the Great Pond you can see the colonnade of the famous Cameron Gallery. This is a long hall glazed on all sides and surrounded by a covered gallery which is formed by rows of Ionic columns. Between the columns there are two rows of bronze busts of ancient thinkers, orators, political figures and military leaders, which are mostly copies of antique originals, and also a sculptural portrait of the Russian scientist Mikhail Lomonosov, cast from a model by his friend, the sculptor Fedot Shubin, which is believed to be a very good likeness of the original.

The Cameron Gallery has its broad, solemn-looking main staircase towards the Grotto. The staircase is ornamented with statues of Hercules Farnesius famous for his noble spirit, strength and valour (the original, the work of Lysippus, a 4th-century B.C. Greek sculptor, has not survived, but a later Roman copy of the statue was located in the collection of a noble Italian family, the Farnese, and from this the statue takes its name) and of Flora. The Russian sculptor Fyodor Gordeyev took the mould for casting these statues from the antique originals in 1786. During the occupation of the town of Pushkin these statues were plundered by the Nazis. But they were fortunately discovered in the German city of Halle outside a copper smeltery waiting to be melted down along with a lot of scrap metal. In 1947 they were returned to Pushkin and after restoration returned to their pedestals at the Cameron Gallery.

Ramp.
Agate Rooms Pavilion.
Interior.

From the gallery you come out into the **Hanging Gardens**, which rest on a platform supported by thick stone columns. The platform is covered with sheets of lead on which there is a sufficiently thick layer of earth for flowers, shrubs and even trees to grow.

Also facing the Hanging Gardens is one of the façades of the **Agate Rooms**. This is a pavilion which was so named on account of its interior being faced with this semiprecious stone, the agate. At the entrance to the Agate Rooms there is a portico in the form of a rotunda covered by a flat dome and in the niches are allegories of the four elements — water, air, earth, and fire. The pavilion consists of two floors. On the ground floor there was a bathing pool with a comparatively plain interior décor, while the first floor is considerably more splendid, being ornamented with paintings, mouldings and bronzes.

The Agate Rooms shared the same sad fate as many of the other monuments of culture at Pushkin. During the occupation the pavilion was used as a stable and the Nazis carried off the agate, jasper and bronze.

From the Hanging Gardens you descend into the park down the **Ramp**, a gently sloping stone walk supported by arches of porous, rough-surface stone, which is an integral part of the architectural ensemble designed by Cameron. The arched vaults of the Ramp are ornamented with masks of mythological gods and heroes. On the Ramp stand decorative vases in the form of ancient sacrificial vessels.

The Ramp was built on the initiative of Catherine the Great, who was averse to using stairways. To the north of the Ramp (and to the west of the palace) there is a charming green nook which was fenced off in the 19th century to be used by the royal family and which came to be known as the **Private Garden**. Incidentally, in the second half of the 18th century this garden was a favourite recreation haunt of Catherine the Great. Here you can see the Kagulski obelisk of beautiful proportions by Antonio Rinaldi, commemorating Russia's victories over Turkey in the war of 1768-1774, the first one to have been put up at Tsarskoye Selo.

At the end of the 18th century this place was an open meadow and by the mid-19th century paths were laid, flowers and shrubs plated, a marble fountain put up and a pergola, a gallery with greenery growing in it which has survived to this day, was built in the Private Garden.

Agate Rooms Pavilion.
Staircase.

The terrace was built in 1808-1810 by Luigi Rusca from pink and grey granite. Fifty years later it was ornamented with statues which were copies of antique originals. In the centre of the square in front of the terrace is a statue of Apollo Belvedere. From the Granite Terrace a path leads to the shore of the Great Pond. On an artificial islet in the centre of this vast reservoir is the building of the **Concert Hall** which is partly covered by the trees. Originally built in the mid-18th century to the design of Rastrelli it was later altered more than once both by Giacomo Quarenghi and Vassili Stasov. Usually an orchestra performed here. The musicians played horns, each tuned to a certain note, yet their performance was perfectly coordinated. The music they played was heard all over the pond, delighting the ears of the courtiers as they relaxed in their boats on the Great Pond. Beyond this pavilion on another artificial islet which is shaped like a truncated pyramid the **Chesma Column** rises high above the water. This commemorates the brilliant victory won by the Russian fleet over the Turkish navy in the Chesma Bay of the Aegean Sea on the night of June 26, 1770. This 25 metre high column of multicoloured marble and granite, ornamented with rostrums, was built by Antonio Rinaldi between 1771 and 1778. It is crowned by a bronze eagle (the symbol of Russia).

On the shore of the Great Pond below the Granite Terrace is a miniature landing stage ornamented with two bronze copies of antique statues. Not far from it the trees and shrubs lining the shore walk give way to a beautiful little square in the centre of which stands what is, perhaps, the most famous adornment of the Catherine Park — the *Milkmaid Fountain*, which was immortalized by Pushkin in his poem. The composition depicts a girl sitting sadly on the rocks, holding a fragment of a broken milk jug that lies by her feet. From the cracked neck of the jug a stream of water pours into a tiny bowl that had been hollowed out of the granite. The fountain was built in 1816 by the sculptor Pavel Sokolov, who succeeded in creating a poetic composition full of deep sadness... Ahead in the southwestern corner of the Great Pond you can see the blue and white **Marble Bridge** which runs across the channel connecting the Great Pond with a number of smaller ponds and channels.

The Marble Bridge, also known as the Siberian Bridge, was built by Vassili Neyelov between 1770 and 1776. It is quite reminiscent of one of the works of the Italian architect Andrea Palladio (1508-1580), a predecessor of neoclassicism in architecture. The bridge's gallery, made of blue and white marble, is classically restrained and perfect in form. It is ornamented by beautifully placed Ionic columns and an elegant marble balustrade. Beyond the Marble Bridge is a rather strange-looking structure. It is the granite *Pyramid*, an original summerhouse built by Charles Cameron in 1781.

Not far from it on a small peninsula jutting out into the Great Pond stands a distinctive pavilion built by Ippolit Monighetti in 1852. It is the **Turkish Baths**, erected on the orders of Nicholas I in commemoration of the Russo-Turkish war of 1828-1829. The building which actually did function as a Turkish bath resembles a mosque. The moulded ornamentation round the doors and on the dome is not the product of Monighetti's imagination, but an exact reproduction of sketches of places of worship which he made during a trip to Turkey. The interiors of the pavilion were decorated in the Moorish style. This pavilion suffered badly during the Nazi occupation of Pushkin. Outside it has been restored, but the restoration work on its interiors is still far from completion.

At the far end of the alley running from the centre of the Catherine Palace is the remarkable masterpiece of Russian architecture which echoes the palace in colour.

Northwest of the Private Garden the yellow-and-white building of the pavilion known as the **Evening Hall** is to be seen through the foliage of the trees. This modest and austere structure built by the architect Ilya Neyelov at the turn of the 19th century incorporates the finest traditions of Russian classicism. The entrance to the hall is ornamented with Ionic pilasters and its windows, with caryatids. The hall was intended to be used as a ballroom. Only selected guests were invited to the dancing parties that were held here. Today various exhibitions are periodically arranged in this pavilion.

The alley which starts at the Ramp and serves as its continuation will take you to the **Granite Terrace**. It is raised high above the surrounding landscape and from here you have a magnificent view over the Great Pond and the area adjoining it. As you can see, this part of the Catherine Park is in the English landscaped and not in the French "regular" style.

The **Hermitage** was built between 1744 and 1756 by Mikhail Zemtsov, Alexei Kvasov, Savva Chevakinsky, and the brilliant Francesco Bartolomeo Rastrelli. The blue colour of its walls alternates with the white of its sixty-four columns standing around the perimeter of the building. The façade of the Hermitage is ornamented with wreaths, masks and shells. During the reign of Elizabeth Petrovna, the daughter of Peter the Great, the Hermitage was even more beautiful than it is today. It was surrounded by a moat with drawbridges and in 1750 the ground from the banks of the moat to the walls of the pavilion was laid with slabs of blue and white marble in a chequered pattern, while an elegant balustrade ornamented with gilded carved wooden figures ran around the moat which was faced in stone. The roof of the Hermitage was also splendidly ornamented at the time.

Today the Hermitage is a much more modest building. Already in the late 18th century the moat around the building was filled in and many of the statues were removed from the façade and the roof on the orders of Catherine the Great.

It should be noted that the kitchen of the Hermitage was not on the ground floor of the building, but it was housed in a single-storied brick building somewhat reminiscent of medieval structures which has survived to this day. In the centre of the Hermitage kitchen, located several dozen metres to the east of the Hermitage, is an archway surmounted with a turret. This archway served as an entrance gate to the Catherine Park.

The path running from the Hermitage kitchen and past the Hermitage will take you to the shore of the Great Pond. Its area is about 16 hectares and it reaches two and a half metres in depth. Work was begun on the building of this reservoir during the first years in which Tsarskoye Selo became a royal residence. In 1770 the outline of its banks was changed and it became the compositional centre of the Catherine Park and the point of connection between its "regular" and landscaped sections.

Here on the shore of the Great Pond is a red-brick Gothic style building with crenellated towers and lancet windows. Next to it are two side wings in the same style. This complex was built by Vassili Neyelov between 1773 and 1777. The building was not designed purely for decorative purposes: it had a definite use. The ground floor of the central building housed a collection of boats, including sealskin-covered Aleutian bidarkas, an Indian dugout, a Turkish kayak, a Venetian gondola, Paul I's boat brought here from Pavlovsk, and other rowing and sailing craft. This boathouse came to be known as the **Admiralty**. The spacious room on the upper floor was a hall the walls of which were faced with glazed tiles and the ceiling decorated with stucco moulding.

In the side wings of the Tsarskoye Selo Admiralty was a poultry house in which peacocks, pheasants and black and white swans were kept. They also housed the living quarters for the sailors and poultry keepers. From the Admiralty a path running along the shore of the pond leads to a light pavilion known as the Grotto.

The **Grotto** was built by Francesco Bartolomeo Rastrelli between 1753 and 1757. Originally its interior was ornamented with coloured seashells. A total of 210,000 large shells and 17.5 poods of (1 pood equals 16.38 kg) of small shells was used for the purpose. In combination with the tufa rock this multi-coloured ornamentation gave the illusion of a fairy-tale cave. Around the top of the Grotto ran an elegant stone balustrade. But as time changes, tastes change too. Catherine the Great ordered the interior décor of the Grotto to be altered in keeping with the neoclassical style. The balustrade was removed, the

Chesma Column. A. Rinaldi's design. 1771-1778.

At the next pages:
Marble Bridge and Concert Hall.

shells taken off and Antonio Rinaldi designed a new interior for the Grotto incorporating the classical style mouldings that have been preserved to this day. But the splendid ornamentation of the Grotto's exterior still makes it possible to get an idea of what Rastrelli's original design looked like. Here all the decorative mouldings are devoted to glorifying the sea element. The wrought-iron door grille of exquisite workmanship made by Russian craftsmen is a superb adornment of the Grotto.

Adjoining the north end of the Catherine Park is the **Alexander Park**. Of the buildings that have survived here the most interesting is the Alexander Palace, the gem of the Alexander Park. It was commissioned by Catherine the Great for her favourite grandson, the future Emperor Alexander I, and built by Giacomo Quarenghi between 1792 and 1796.

Alexander Palace.
Milkmaid Fountain.
Sculptor P. Sokolov. 1816.

The **Alexander Palace** is an outstanding, epoch-making masterpiece of Russian classicism. Whereas the Catherine Palace reflected the prevalence of the baroque in mid-18th century Russian architecture, the Alexander Palace is a monument of the classical style which followed it in the Russian architecture of the late 18th century. In appearance the Alexander Palace is serene and austere and there are no bright colours or excessive mouldings on its main façade. Seen from above, it looks like a somewhat widened letter U — a shape which is often seen among neoclassicist structures — and its side wings project forward markedly. The palace is painted yellow and white and its side wings are attached to it by two rows of a bright and solemn-looking snow-white Corinthian colonnade, which has no parallel in world architecture. In the late 1830s two statues which depict young men playing Russian traditional games of the period were placed in front of the central part of the colonnade. These dynamic bronze sculptures stand out to perfection against the background of the white colonnade.

Egyptian Gates. Architect A. Menelaws. 1830.

Alexander I did not live a long time at this palace, preferring to stay in his chambers at the Catherine Palace. Nicholas I quite often stayed at the Alexander Palace during his summer visits to Tsarskoye Selo. Alexander II did not like this palace, having a preference for the Catherine Palace. The future Emperor Alexander III lived for a short time at the Alexander Palace when he was the heir to the Russian throne. His son, Nicholas II, preferred Peterhof at the beginning of his reign, while after the revolution of 1905-1907 he lived under strong protection at the Alexander Palace, almost never leaving it.

Besides the royal family, a great number of courtiers stayed at the Alexander Palace, just as at many other buildings of Tsarskoye Selo. Under Nicholas II the court of the Romanov House numbered as many as 1,680 persons.

It was at the Alexander Palace that the imperial family stayed in the days of the February revolution of 1917, which resulted in the overthrow of monarchy. It was also here that he was subsequently brought as the arrested ex-monarch. Soon, how-

ever, on the instructions of the Provisional Government Nicholas Romanov and his family were taken out of Tsarskoye Selo and sent to the town of Tobolsk in Siberia.

The interiors of the Alexander Palace were designed by Quarenghi but this original décor was removed on the orders of Nicholas II in almost all the rooms of the palace.

Listed above are only the most valuable monuments of architecture, sculpture and Russian culture which have gone down in the history of Tsarskoye Selo — the town of Pushkin. Their actual number and variety are far greater.

We leave this picturesque town through the arch of the **Egyptian Gates** built in 1829-1830 to the design of the architect Adam Menelaws, who incorporated in them motifs of ancient Egyptian art.

Next to the Egyptian Gates is a statue of Pushkin. This statue, made by the sculptor Leopold Bernstamm in 1912, was put up at this spot almost at the same time as Tsarskoye Selo was renamed Pushkin.

PAVLOVSK

Pavlovsk is only a few kilometres from Pushkin and these two suburbs of St. Petersburg have many things in common. Their biographies are closely bound together.

After Tsarskoye Selo had been built following the construction of Peterhof, a search was undertaken to find suitable spots near this new out-of-town imperial residence for the royal hunt. The area selected was that around which is today's Pavlovsk for here there were elk and other game in abundance. Cavalcades of carefree horsemen and horsewomen galloped up and down the valley... The first buildings to appear in the area were two wooden hunting lodges which were humorously called "Krik" and "Krak".

In 1777 Catherine the Great gave this land to her unloved son, Paul. Soon afterwards in 1782 an obelisk was built by Charles Cameron on the right bank of the quiet and slow-moving river Slavyanka in honour of the founding of Pavlovsk.

His name is also associated with the laying of the park and the design and construction of the Great Palace. The classicist style characteristic of Cameron's works is also to be seen in such structures as the Temple of Friendship, the Monument to Maria Fyodorovna's Parents, the Apollo Colonnade, and others, which were built in the park.

In 1790 Pavlovsk became the official summer residence of Paul I, who had by then become Emperor of Russia. Just as the entire retinue of the late empress, Cameron, who had been highly appraised by Catherine the Great, fell into disfavour under Paul and was taken off the construction work at Pavlovsk.

An adherent of classicism, Cameron was replaced by Vincenzo Brenna, an Italian decorator and architect. He began his work at Pavlovsk with painting the plafonds in the Great Palace and then he extended the palace and built a number of summer-houses and pavilions in the park. Characteristic of Brenna's style was the combination of classicism with its traditional restraint and romanticism with its abundance of ornament. Brenna made the Great Palace more ostentatious in appearance and designed the layout of the Great Circles, one of the sections of the park. At the time such formal sections of the park, very regular in arrangement, as the Old Silvia and the New Silvia were laid. The pavilion called the Pil-Tower was built on the left bank of the Slavyanka. Streets were laid and dwelling houses built near the park.

On November 12, 1796, Emperor Paul I, who had just ascended the throne, renamed the village of Pavlovskoye to the town of Pavlovsk. He was not, however, destined to live at Pavlovsk for a long time. In March 1801 he was assassinated at the Mikhailovsky Castle in St. Petersburg in the course of a palace coup. During the early 19th century the Russian architect, Andrei Voronikhin, took charge of the building at Pavlovsk. He rebuilt the Great Palace after it had been badly damaged during a fire

Pavlovsk Palace.
View from the Slavyanka river.

in 1803 and designed the bridges over the Slavyanka. Besides Voronikhin, Cameron also worked at Pavlovsk at the time, having returned here after the death of Paul I. The great Scotsman built a number of structures, including the charming Pavilion of the Three Graces, which is situated slightly to the south of the Great Palace. The celebrated architect Carlo Rossi, who had built some of the magnificent ensembles at St. Petersburg, made a major contribution to the construction work which was in progress here. At Pavlovsk, however, Rossi did not build any ensembles: his work here was largely confined to designing wrought-iron fences, decorative vases, ferries, a number of summerhouses, and the wrought-iron gates put up at the entrance to Pavlovsk.

We have only given the names of a few great architects. Besides them, however, numerous other masters of palace-and-park architecture and skilful craftsmen who adorned the Great Palace with their priceless artistic masterpieces also worked at Pavlovsk. The gardeners planted various species of trees, carefully calculating the time when their leaves would turn yellow or red under the cold breath of autumn northerly winds, thus creating an inimitable colourful setting for the palace.

Pavlovsk is famous not only for its unique palace and park. In the Pavlovsk concert hall, which was located near the railway station, the celebrated Russian ballet dancer, Anna Pavlova, performed in her day. A year after the Lumière brothers invented cinema (1895) motion pictures were shown in the audi-

torium of the Pavlovsk Kursaal. The Austrian composer and conductor Johann Strauss, the world-famous "king of the waltz", performed here for several years during his tour of Russia.

During the first months of the war with Nazi Germany a total of 12,000 museum pieces were successfully evacuated from Pavlovsk. Many other items such as decorative objects from the Great Palace, statues and other articles of artistic value were either buried in the earth or walled up in the palace cellars.

The Nazis devastated the park, cutting down tens of thousands of trees which they used in building fortifications. Many of the beautiful pavilions of the Pavlovsk park such as the Pink Pavilion, the Krik and the Old Chalet and all the bridges over the Slavyanka were blown up and destroyed. The palace itself was also blown up.

Photographs of the ruins of this remarkable architectural monument were shown in evidence by the prosecution among other documents at the Nuremberg Trial of Nazi war criminals.

On January 24, 1944, Pavlovsk was liberated. Restoration work was started here. The Great Palace was resurrected from charred ruins and more than 60,000 trees were planted in the park.

The **Pavlovsk Park**, one of the largest parks in the world, covers an area of more than 600 hectares. Both geometrical and landscape planning have been used here according to the character of the country in Pavlovsk, which consists largely of undulating hills and valleys through which the meandering Slavyanka flows.

Pavlovsk Palace.
Detail of the Main Façade.

PAVLOVSK PALACE

The main structure at Pavlovsk is the Great Palace (Pavlovsk Palace). This is the compositional centre of the park and it can be seen from its farthest parts. This three-storied stone building, which seems to be soaring above the valley of the Slavyanka, impresses you by the combination of monumental size and lightness. Sixty-four white columns placed close to one another support the flat cupola which crowns the building. The ground floor is designed as a monumental plinth on which the two upper floors rest. The ground floor with its state rooms clearly dominates over the ground floor, which contained the living quarters, and over the second floor where the rooms were more modest.

Whereas from the northeast (i.e. from the Slavyanka River) the Great Palace looks just like a magnificent country residence, from the southeast (i.e. from the main entrance) this imposing horseshoe-shaped building has none of the simplicity and homeliness associated with country residences, but rather all the ostentation of the official residence of Emperor Paul I.
The central building of the palace with galleries was built by Charles Cameron between 1782 and 1786. Subsequently in 1786-1800 Vincenzo Brenna added the side wings and completed the interiors of the state rooms. In 1800, Giacomo Quarenghi took part in decorating a number of the interiors. Later on, Andrei Voronikhin and also Carlo Rossi, who designed the Library, worked on the interior décor of the palace.

Pavlovsk Palace:
Egyptian Vestibule.
Italian Hall. Detail of the door décor.
Paul I's Lesser Study. Clock. Charpentier studio (Paris).
Marble, gilded bronze. Second half of the 18th century.

PAVLOVSK PALACE: INTERIOR

The first of the palace's exquisitely and variously decorated rooms is the *Egyptian Vestibule*. The original vestibule was the work of Charles Cameron and the outstanding Russian sculptor, Ivan Prokofyev. The twelve statues symbolizing the months of the year which adorned the vestibule were damaged during a fire in 1803 and replaced by others, made from sketches by Voronikhin, which were based on artistic motifs from ancient Egypt that were in vogue at the time. At the foot of each bronze-coated statue there are various tools and implements such as might be used in the corresponding months. Above the statues are medallions containing the signs of the zodiac. The painting on the ceiling, made in grisaille giving the effect of sculpture in relief, depicts cupids symbolizing the four seasons. Another superb feature of this room is crystal chandeliers reminiscent of bells in shape.

The staircase with elegant wrought-iron banisters made in the baroque style takes you up to the *Main Vestibule* on the first floor. Designed by Vincenzo Brenna in 1790, the vestibule is richly ornamented with mouldings, chiefly in the form of accoutrements. The carved wooden standard lamps standing in the vestibule are also in the same style. The room is divided by a broad arch with square recesses which are filled with bronze-coated mouldings. The arch is supported by towering Atlases. Panels by the staircase depict Russian military standards, and also Turkish turbans and staffs which were the attributes of the Turkish generals. These motifs recall Russia's victories in the Russo-Turkish War (second half of the 18th century).

Adjoining the Main Vestibule on its northwestern side is the magnificent *Italian Hall*, which was the first room in the palace where restoration work was started after the liberation of Pavlovsk. The hall is located in the centre of the palace and it is illuminated with the natural light which enters through the apertures in the cupola crowning the palace building. The original interior of this central state room of the palace was designed by Vincenzo Brenna in 1789, but after suffering damage during the fire of 1803 it was redesigned by Andrei Voronikhin. The eagles on the cornice of the cupola and the caryatids which support it are his work.

The walls of the hall are faced with lilac and pink artificial marble. The beautifully patterned stone floor and the streams of light which pour down from the ceiling give the room a distinct similarity to the atria in the palaces of ancient Rome, which is why it is known as the Italian Hall. The hall is circular and divided vertically into three sections. This division is emphasized along the horizontals by gilded moulded cornices. The gallery and cupola help give the room a ceremonial appearance. Note the beautiful chandelier of Russian workmanship. It is made of bronze and ruby glass and has very unusual "ostrich feathers" made of crystal. The walls of the hall are decorated with antique marble bas-reliefs. Here too there are some genuine examples of 1st and 2nd century A.D. Roman sculpture such as "Venus with a Dove", "Faun Playing a Flute", "The Dancing Satyr", and "Eros Stringing His Bow".

The collection of antique sculptural works at the Pavlovsk Palace is second in richness only to that at the Hermitage in St. Petersburg. Some of these sculptures at one time were part of the famous collection of antiques which belonged to Lord Hamilton (British ambassador to Naples). They were purchased by Catherine the Great.

The state rooms of Paul I — the northern enfilade of the palace — begin with the comparatively modest *Valet's Room*. Here the duty officer would sit during royal receptions awaiting the emperor's call. Next along is the *Dressing Room*, which was designed by Cameron as a rectangular room with rounded corners and a vaulted ceiling. The walls of this elegant room are covered with mouldings and paintings depicting jasmine garlands. The soft tones of the paintings combine well with the exquisite low-relief mouldings. Of note here is the antique sculpture "Faun and Panther" (2nd century A.D.) standing by the window. Next to it is a palm-wood dressing table made in 1784.

From the Dressing Room you pass through a modestly decorated room called the *Communicating Room*. The carved gilded furniture was made from poplar in 1825 to Carlo Rossi's design. The room is ornamented with pictures by Russian painters Semyon Shchedrin and Andrei Martynov, showing views of the Pavlovsk Park as it was in the late 18th century.

The next room along is the *Library*, a large and slightly curved hall lighted through five large semicircular windows. This room was added to the palace by Rossi in 1824 to accommodate the palace library. Before the war there were bookcases here which were decorated with carving so that they seemed to be ornamented with bronze.

The bookcases contained over 20,000 volumes comprising the palace library. Besides, on the tables and in the showcases that were in this room there were collections of engravings, sketches and drawings. Many of these books and drawings were saved, but the beautiful furniture of the Library was destroyed during a fire in 1944.

Also adjoining the Dressing Room is *Paul I's Lesser Study*. On one of its walls is a full-length portrait of Peter the Great with a battle scene in the background. It is believed to be the work of Johann Gottfried Tannauer, an artist who was invited to Russia by Peter the Great from Saxony. On particular interest are the distinctive 18th-century French writing desk, the grandfather clock decorated with masonic signs, and the mahogany screen by the fire-place which is inlaid with ivory and copies of antique cameos. The chandelier made by Pierre-Joseph-Désiré Gouthière, the famous French maker of bronzes is also an excellent piece of workmanship.

Pavlovsk Palace:
Paul I's Library.
Communicating Room.

Next along is *Paul I's Library*. It was built to the design of Vincenzo Brenna in the 1790s and restored after the fire of 1803 by Andrei Voronikhin. Its walls are faced with artificial white marble and hung with Gobelin tapestries, made in Paris, which are decorated with themes from the fables of La Fontaine. These woven pictures were presented to Paul I in 1782 (while he was still the heir to the throne) by Louis XVI of France. The full-dress portrait of Maria Fyodorovna, the wife of Paul I, was painted in 1794 by the Austrian painter J. Lampi. In the centre of the room is a large mahogany writing desk edged in bronze. On it are elegant candelabra and a desk set made of amber and ivory, all of which were made in St. Petersburg to the design of Brenna.

Along the walls there are low white bookcases on which marble sculptures are placed.

Among these sculptures is an interesting work by the outstanding Russian sculptor, Mikhail Kozlovsky, entitled "Sleeping Cupid and the Club of Hercules".

103

Pavlovsk Palace:
Tapestry Study.
Hall of Peace.

The next room is the *Tapestry Study*, the walls of which are adorned with Gobelin tapestries from a series representing motifs from Cervantes' novel "Don Quixote". The four tapestries from this series, made at the royal manufactory in Paris, were a present to Paul I from Louis XVI. These Gobelin tapestries with a pink and crimson background are truly unique. The furniture is also beautiful here. It includes a mahogany writing desk inlaid with ivory, which was intended for Paul I's study at the Mikhailovsky Castle in St. Petersburg, and a carved and gilded suite ornamented with Lyons embroidery, which was made in 1784 by the famous Parisian cabinet-maker, Georges Jacob. Also of note are the marble sculpture, the various amber and ivory ornaments, the beautiful clock, and the Japanese and French porcelain vases.

The last room along this enfilade is the *Hall of War*. For a short time after Paul I's ascent to the throne, this room was used as a small throne room. Although not particularly large in size, this room was highly suitable for ceremonial occasions, being faced in white artificial marble and having gilded mouldings and representations of ancient Roman weapons and armour on the walls which give it a certain majestic atmosphere. In the lunettes (arched openings in the ceiling) are bas-reliefs depicting scenes from the Trojan War. The niches in this octagonal hall contain antique marble busts of Roman emperors.

The *Hall of Peace* is symmetrical to the Hall of War with respect to the Grecian Hall. Octagonal in shape it has four splendidly decorated niches in one of which is a beautifully ornamented stove. Instead of the fearsome eagle, which crowns the stove in the Hall of War, here in the Hall of Peace there is Juno's peacock (Juno was the Roman queen of the gods and goddess of marriage). The layout of this Hall is very similar to that of the Hall of War.

But here there are no military paraphernalia, their place being taken by symbols of peaceful pursuits such as agricultural implements, baskets of flowers and fruit, bunches of grapes, and musical instruments. Although on the gilded doors there are bows and quivers full of arrows, these are not intended as weapons of war but as symbols of love aiming for peace.

In the Hall of Peace there is an exceptionally finely proportioned tripod vase of crystal and golden-red glass which was designed by Andrei Voronikhin and made in 1811. It is one of the finest works of applied art to be seen at the Pavlovsk Palace.

Along the perimeter of the palace runs the state enfilade — a chain of rectangular rooms superbly decorated in the classicist style. They include the famous *Grecian Hall*, one of the main halls in the Pavlovsk Palace. It was built by Vinzenco Brenna in 1789 and after the fire of 1803 it was renewed by Andrei Voronikhin. The room is designed to resemble a Greek peristyle. But the fine greenish artificial marble columns that stand out against the smooth walls faced with artificial white marble make it also look something like an ancient Greek temple. In the niches are copies of classical sculptures. The entablature above the columns and the ceiling are adorned with fine moulding. Two slender six-sided lamps of gilded bronze and marble lamps hanging on long chains between the columns complete the ornamentation of the Grecian Hall.

Note the beautiful vases, clocks and candelabra on the marble fireplaces and console tables and the magnificently embroidered curtains, which were made in Paris in 1782. Hung in the Grecian Hall of the Pavlovsk Palace as soon as they arrived here, these latter had become rather worn by the mid-19th century so they were taken down and for more than 100 years lay in one of the palace's storerooms. After the war Soviet specialists restored the work of the French weavers.

Today the Grecian Hall is often used for giving concerts for lovers of chamber music.

The windows of the Hall of War, the Grecian Hall and the Hall of Peace afford an enchanting view of the Slavyanka and its banks stretching before the northwestern façade of the palace, and from the western window of the Hall of Peace you can see a beautiful panorama of the cascade which flows from the Apollo Colonnade down its stony channel to the waters of the Slavyanka River.

The next room after the Hall of Peace is the *Library of Maria Fyodorovna*. On its central wall there is another Don Quixote tapestry, made in 1780. Around the walls of the room stand white bookcases, which also serve as consoles for the marble sculptures — 18th-century Italian copies of antique originals with the exception of the sculpture entitled "Muse by the Rock", the one near the windows, which is genuinely Roman, dating from the 2nd century A.D. In the curve formed in the wall there is a mahogany and bronze writing desk, which was made in 1784. At the desk there is a large chair ornamented with cornucopias which served as little vases for flowers and elegantly embroidered upholstery. The restored 18th-century carpetlike patterned parquet is truly magnificent. It is made of twelve different sorts of wood including amaranth, rosewood, mahogany, palm and other woods brought from Intia, Ceylon and other tropical countries. Completing the decor of the room is a crystal chandelier of Russian workmanship which hangs on chains of gilded bronze.

*Pavlovsk Palace
Grecian Hall.*

Pavlovsk Palace:
Boudoir.
Desk with the views of the Pavlovsk Park.
Library of Maria Fyodorovna.

Attached to this room is the small *Boudoir* (by Brenna and Voronikhin). Its main feature is a fireplace of white Carrara marble ornamented with gilded bronze and porphyry. It has the shape of a classical portal. The classical forms of the fireplace harmonize with the 18th-century pilasters made in Rome which are decorated in motifs from Raphael's paintings in the Loggias of the Vatican. Between the pilasters there are ancient Roman bas-reliefs and medallions of marble with portraits of Alexander the Great and his mother, Olympia. Of note among the furniture in the Boudoir is a table made at the St. Petersburg porcelain factory in 1789 on whose porcelain top are depicted views of the Pavlovsk Park. The piano which is to be seen here was made in London in 1774. Note also the lamp of bronze and green glass which hangs on long chains. It was specially designed by Voronikhin for the Boudoir.

Pavlovsk Palace.
State Bedchamber.
Couch and plafond.

The next room is the nearly square-shaped *State Bedchamber*. Actually it was never used as a bedroom and only included in the enfilade in keeping with the palace traditions. The walls are hung with silk decorated with a pattern of flowers, fruits and musical instruments. One of the main features of this room is a fireplace made of white Carrara marble with malachite pilasters. The magnificent four-poster bed which is ornamented with delicate carving showing baskets of flowers and the altar of love with doves and cupids, together with the couch and chairs were made by Georges Jacob on commission from Paul I. On a special table in a display case is the 64-piece toilet service of Sèvres porcelain which was commissioned by Marie Antoinette, the wife of Louis XVI, and presented by the queen to the wife of Paul I during her stay in France in 1782. It includes objects ornamented with embossed rolled gold and enamel inserts in imitation of precious stones. The bisque sculptures holding the mirror are made from a model by Louis-Simon Boizot. The three-legged tables of gilded bronze, lapis lazuli and marble are approximate copies of the antique originals found in the ruins of Pompeii.

110

Next to the State Bedchamber is *Maria Fyodorovna's Dressing Room*. Its interior decor was designed by Vincenzo Brenna in 1797. The walls of this small room are faced with artificial white marble and divided into numerous panels which are ornamented with fine decorative moulding by the outstanding Russian sculptor, Ivan Prokofyev. The restraint of the geometrical pattern combines well with the rich floral ornament and the scenes from classical mythology. On the walls of the Dressing Room are wall panels showing views of the Pavlovsk Park — the Temple of Friendship and the Great Cascade. Of particular interest in this room is the "steel toilet set". It includes a dressing table with a mirror, vases, candlesticks, a footstool and a chair which are made up of several thousand metal parts all given what was called a "steel diamond" finish. This unique set was made in 1788 by Semyon Samarin, a worker at the Tula armoury.

At the end of the enfilade is a small *Room for the Ladies-in-Waiting*, who used to stand here waiting for the entrance of the empress from her inner chambers. Of note in this room is the late 18th-century carved and gilded suite of Russian workmanship and a statue by Louis-Simon Boizot showing a vestal bearing sacrifice (in ancient Rome the vestal virgins were the priestesses of Vesta, the goddess of the hearth, who tended the sacred fire in her temple). Also of interest in the Ladies-in-Waiting Room is the bronze clock which stands on the mahogany bureau. It depicts a scene from Monsigny's opera, "The Deserter", which was popular in its time in court circles. The clock incorporates a music box which plays tunes from the opera every hour on the hour. The clock was out of operation for 150 years and has been revived by the skilful restorers at the Pavlovsk Palace-Museum.

The state rooms take up not only the main building of the palace but they continue in the semicircular galleries and the left side wing.

The *First Communicating Room* opens the route from the central part of the palace to its western rooms built by Brenna. Of note in this room is the marble fireplace with a mirror in a gilded frame which is decorated with porcelain vases made in Germany in the second half of the 18th century.

Following it is the *Second Communicating Room*, faced with artificial pink marble. Porcelain vases made by Russian craftsmen stand in the niches. The 18th-century Italian sculpture depicts a scene from a classical myth which describes how an eagle, sent by Zeus, abducted Ganymede and carried him off to Mount Olympus where Ganymede became the cupbearer to the gods. Of note here is also the late 18th-century French escritoire which is adorned with a clock ornamented with enamels, made in Liège.

From here you pass into the arc-shaped *Picture Gallery*. Among the masterpieces on display in this room are a sketch of "Pietà" by the great Rubens and the "Expulsion from the Garden of Eden" by the outstanding 17th-century Italian master Luca Giordano.

From the Picture Gallery you enter the *Third Communicating Room*. Its walls are faced with marble of warm lilac hue and ornamented by panels with glass insets which are covered with decorative painting. During the restoration of Pavlovsk in the postwar years the Soviet artist Anatoli Treskin made a superb representation of the plafond which was originally the work of Pietro Gonzago. This plafond, which shows arcades receding upwards, makes the room look higher, thus creating an effective artistic transition to the next room, the Throne Hall, which has a greater height.

The *Throne Hall* is the largest (400 square metres) and the most solemn-looking room in the Pavlovsk Palace. It was built by Brenna in 1798 and designed for official ceremonies and receptions. Originally it was called the Great Hall, but soon after it was built, Paul I's throne was placed here, which gave rise to the name Throne Hall. In the reign of Alexander I, Paul I's son, a ceremonial reception was given in this hall for the Guards generals and officers who had returned home after the victory over Napoleon's Grande Armée and the seizure of Paris. On that occasion the throne was removed from the hall and was never put back.

Square in shape, its four corners are rounded off to form deep niches with decorative heating stoves. Its white marble walls offer an impressive contrast with the polished mahogany doors and the luxurious gilded candelabra. The arches supported by caryatids further emphasize the solemn appearance of the room. Originally created by the sculptors Ivan Martos and Mikhail Kozlovsky, the caryatids perished in a fire and were restored under the supervision of the Soviet sculptor I. Krestovsky. On the ceiling is a perspective-emphasizing plafond painted by Soviet masters under the supervision of Anatoli Treskin from surviving sketches by Pietro Gonzago.

Leading off the southwestern wall of the Throne Hall are two service rooms. The first of these, the northern one, is the *Orchestral Chamber* where the court musicians sat by the mirror door opening on to the Throne Hall when they played at royal receptions and balls.

Next to the Orchestral Chamber is the *Pantry*, from which the servants brought out dishes to the table during receptions. Today it houses a display of some of the dinner and tea services which were used during formal receptions and which were in everyday use at the Pavlovsk Palace. The bronze chandelier which is adorned with a bouquet of lilies of the valley made of crystal hanging in this room is very beautiful. It was made by Russian craftsmen in the 18th century.

The Orchestral Chamber adjoins the long rectangular *Knights' Hall*. Built to the design of Vincenzo Brenna in 1798, it was intended for holding ceremonial receptions for the Knights of Malta.

Pavlovsk Palace:
Orchestral Chamber. Detail.
Knights' Hall.

The Knights' Hall is ornamented with mouldings and bas-reliefs depicting Bacchic dances, ceremonial processions and sacrifices. The plafond, designed by Brenna, imitates the moulded ornamentation of the ceiling. The hall houses a collection of 2nd and 3rd century A.D. classical sculptures.

From the Knights' Hall you may enter the *Palace Church* or, rather, its choir loft. Of interest here are the white and golden standard lamps and the 18th-century silver chandelier.

The door in the far end of the Knights' Hall leads into the *Horseguards' Room*. This was the headquarters of the Palace Guard. Guarding the palace was the duty of the officers of the Horseguards Regiment.

It is best to begin your tour of the ground floor, where the masters of the Pavlovsk Palace lived, with the *Ballroom*. Its pink and light blue tints provide an intimate atmosphere, an impression which is enhanced by the delicate gilded mouldings, the elegant springs of flowers and the classical vases. In this hall there are four paintings by the outstanding 18th-century French artist, Hubert Robert, who painted mostly classical ruins and who was very much in fashion in his day.

On the right of the Ballroom is the *French Chamber* decorated with large Gobelin tapestries presented by Louis XVI to Paul I in 1782. On the left of the Ballroom, beyond the Old Drawing Room, is the *Billiard Room*. In this corner room there are skilfully ornamented card tables made by Russian craftsmen in the second half of the 18th century. Of note here is also the clavicord-cum-organ, a unique musical instrument, which was commissioned by Catherine the Great and made in St. Petersburg in 1783. Originally it stood in the Taurida Palace, which was a gift from the empress to Prince Potemkin, her favourite. Although it is called the Billiard Room there is no billiard table here. This is because it was removed in the mid-19th century to Strelna, another royal residence in the environs of St. Petersburg, and never returned to Pavlovsk, having been lost.

At the next pages:
Palace Church.

On the left of the Billiard Room is the *Dining Hall*, which is the largest room on the ground floor. The decor here, which is the work of Charles Cameron, is solemn and austere. White fluted pilasters stand out effectively against the pistachio green of the walls, around which runs an elegant moulded frieze with figures of cupids, lions, vases, and floral ornamentation. The French windows offer a splendid view of the valley of the Slavyanka River.

Here the royal family and their close friends from among the courtiers dined. Displayed on the table is one of the biggest and most famous dinner services to be seen in the royal residences. It was made at the St. Petersburg porcelain factory in the early 19th century.

To the left of the Dining Hall is the *Corner Chamber*. It was restored after the war from surviving fragments and drawings by Carlo Rossi, who designed the interior. Rossi, however, did not confine himself to the architectural decor of this room. The wavy-birch suite with its gilded carving, the bronze and coloured crystal chandelier and the distinctive curtains which are to be seen here were also made to his design. The walls are faced with violet and lilac artificial marble and decorated with imitation bronze ornamentation. The painted plafond with its classical masks harmonizes well with this.

The next one in the ground floor suite of private chambers is *Paul I's New Study*. Its walls faced with lilac-pinkish artificial marble are divided into small panels in narrow frames of gilded moulding. The decor of the walls is enriched by insets of white marble with arabesques and watercolours reminiscent of Raphael's paintings in the Loggias at the Vatican in miniature. The

beautiful white marble fireplace is ornamented with bas-reliefs. This room was decorated in 1800 to the design of Giacomo Quarenghi. The mahogany and bronze furniture in this room is the work of the famous German cabinet-maker, David Röntgen. Next along is the *Common Room*, where Paul I's family used to gather. Here there are portraits of members of the emperor's family by outstanding 18th- and early 19th-century Russian and West European portraitists. The mahogany furniture in the room is in the Jacob style (after Georges-Alphonse Jacob, the French cabinet-maker, who was the first to use fluted brass in ornamenting furniture). The bronze and mahogany bureau is by David Röntgen. It was brought to Russia in 1786. In the room there are many desktop ornaments made of amber and ivory such as obelisks, desk sets and candelabra.

Adjoining the Common Room is the *Old Study*, also called the *Crimson Study*, from the colour of the upholstery and curtains. Of interest here in addition to the landscapes which are to be seen in this room is the mosaic depicting the Coliseum in Rome, which was a present to Paul I given him by Pope Pius VI in 1782.

Pavlovsk Palace:
Pilaster Study.
Bedchamber.
Lantern Room.

An elongated *Antechamber* leads from the main part of the palace to its western wing, which was built by Giacomo Quarenghi and Andrei Voronikhin. Beyond the Antechamber is the round *Valet's Chamber* which was the seat of the duty valet during audiences given by the emperor. From the Valet's Chamber you enter a much larger room, the *Pilaster Study*.

The interior of the Pilaster Study was decorated to the design of Quarenghi in 1800. The room derives its name from the golden-yellow artificial marble pilasters crowned with Corinthian capitals. The decor of the study is fully in keeping with the traditions of classicism. The white marble and golden pilasters contrast well with the dark bas-reliefs and give the room an austere and solemn look. The mahogany suite in this room was designed by Voronikhin and made by the well-known St. Petersburg cabinet-maker, Heinrich Gambs. The two jasper vases on either side of the bureau were made at a lapidary factory in the Urals in 1802.

You next come to one of the most charming rooms in the palace, the *Lantern Room*, which was designed by Voronikhin in 1807. The glass panelled wall of the room projects out into the garden (in the shape of a lantern) and is surmounted with a vault which rests on elegant Ionic columns faced with artificial white marble. The lacunars in the vault are ornamented with camomile-shaped rosettes. On either side of the arch at its foot are caryatids, which are the work of the sculptor Vassili Demut-Malinovsky. The abundance of light filling the Lantern Room

Pavilion of the Three Graces.
Ch. Cameron's design. 1800.

lends it an atmosphere of lightness and airiness. The black and gold furniture designed by Voronikhin harmonizes beautifully with the overall design of the room. Many of the paintings which are to be seen here were purchased in Italy with the aid of the artist Orest Kiprensky.

Besides the writing desk and the other pieces of furniture there are a number of fine works of applied art made to Voronikhin's design such as the round crystal table and the three-legged table with a blue glass top.

The next room along is the *Dressing Room*, designed by Quarenghi in 1800. The plafond here was painted in the grisaille style giving the illusion of depth with the minimum use of colour. The toilet articles in this room, in particular, the washing set designed by Voronikhin which includes a glass washbowl and a glass pitcher with a tall gilded bronze handle, are very beautiful. They stand on a blue and orange (or, rather, amber) glass table. Amber-coloured glass is also to be seen on the bodies of the vases standing on the bureau. There is a magnificent 34-piece green porcelain toilet service, which is truly an outstanding achievement of Russian pottery.

Next you come to still another room of Voronikhin's design, the *Bedchamber*, with its ceiling and walls attractively decorated with painting showing bright garlands of flowers. The furniture

here was designed by Voronikhin, but part of it — the armchairs and the tabourets — perished in the war and was restored by Soviet masters in 1959. The mahogany and bronze chests of drawers of French workmanship are truly magnificent. Above the divan is a tapestry portrait of Paul I which was made by serf weavers at the St. Petersburg tapestry factory in 1799.

The last room in the northwestern enfilade on the ground floor is the small oval-shaped *Marquee*, which was used by the ladies for resting and needlework.

Near the western façade of the palace is the small *Private Garden* which is laid out according to the style of Dutch formal gardens. The path leading from the palace to the Pavilion of the Three Graces is decorated with vases of white marble placed on coloured marble pedestals. In places the path is covered with trellis arches on which creeping plants are trained. The main adornment of the Private Garden is the **Pavilion of the Three Graces** which was built to the design of Charles Cameron in 1800 right by the edge of the garden. The pavilion is a covered terrace with 16 white Ionic columns under festive-looking flat pediments.

In 1803 a sculptural group, the Three Graces, made by Paolo Triscorni from a single block of marble was placed in the centre of the pavilion.

From the Private Garden the *Stone Staircase* designed by Vincenzo Brenna descends to the bank of the Slavyanka. It consists of 64 steps and at the top and the bottom is adorned with sculptures of lions (those at the top are made of marble and those at the bottom, of iron). The top landing is decorated with vases on pedestals from which balustrades begin.

Turning right along the bank of the Slavyanka you come to another fine pavilion, the **Temple of Friendship**, built by Charles Cameron in 1782 in the classical style. Its name originates from the sentimentalists who were the dominant school of literature in the late 18th century. The Temple is round in shape and it looks like a rotunda with a colonnade of 16 fluted Doric columns surrounding it. Between the columns there are moulded bas-reliefs and under the cornice there is a moulded frieze of garlands and dolphins (the dolphin was a symbol of friendship). The pavilion is topped with a flat cupola, the centre of which is glass admitting light to its inner space. The structure harmonizes beautifully with its surroundings. The columns are reflected in the quiet waters of the Slavyanka and the trees here are planted not to conceal the Temple of Friendship but rather to emphasize its connection with the surrounding landscape. For this reason the Temple of Friendship can be seen even from remote parts of the Pavlovsk Park.

Temple of Friendship.
Ch. Cameron's design. 1782.
Pil-Tower. 1797.

Centaur Bridge.

Leading to the other bank of the Slavyanka is the **Centaur Bridge** built by Nikita Yakovlev, a Russian stonemason, from light stone and fitted with openwork wrought-iron railings. In 1805 Voronikhin placed marble statues of centaurs, made by an Italian master in the late 18th century, at its four corners. During the war they were destroyed by the Nazis and the statues that you see on the bridge are copies of the centaurs cast in epoxy resin. Near the Centaur Bridge on the bank of the Slavyanka is a small pavilion called the **Cold Bath**, where the royal family performed their ablutions in hot weather.

A little further along is the **Apollo Colonnade**, built to the design of Charles Cameron in 1783. Originally it took the form of a double circular colonnade, but during a heavy storm in 1817 part of the colonnade collapsed. Subsequently the damaged part of the colonnade was not restored and the fallen columns were placed by the statue of Apollo Belvedere, thereby giving the whole structure the effect of an ancient ruin. (The classical original of this statue of the mythological sun god and the supreme patron of the arts is in Belvedere, a court in the Vatican, the seat of the Pope of Rome). The Statue of Apollo is put on a high pedestal in the centre of the colonnade which is built of light stone whose deposits are found in the environs of St. Petersburg.

The colonnade is beautifully proportioned and seems to be all light and air. Situated near the palace from where it could be clearly seen, the colonnade was intended to emphasize the royal family's patronage of the arts and their flourishing at Pavlovsk under the aegis of Apollo Belvedere.

In the centre of its part known as the **Old Silvia**, that is, "old forest tract", there is a rigidly geometric, formal area which is called the **Twelve Paths**. Entering the low stone gates you come to a square round which there are 12 bronze statues which were cast at the St. Petersburg Academy of Arts from ancient originals. The statues run clockwise in the following order: Euterpe (the Muse of music and lyric poetry), Melpomene (the Muse of tragedy), Thalia (the Muse of comedy and pastoral poetry), Terpsichore (the Muse of dancing), Erato (the Muse of erotic lyric poetry), Mercury (the messenger of the gods, god of commerce and travel), Venus Callipyge (the goddess of love and beauty), Polyhymnia (the Muse of sacred poetry), Calliope (the Muse of eloquence and epic poetry), Clio (the Muse of history), Urania (the Muse of astronomy), and Flora (the goddess of flowers). In the centre of the circle stands a statue of Apollo, the sun god and protector of the Muses.

From this round square twelve paths run radially outwards. One of them, running west, leads to a pavilion which is called the **Monument to Maria Fyodorovna's Parents** built by Ch. Cameron. This structure is built in the shape of a semicircular temple the inner space of which is separated from the entrance by two Doric columns of pink marble. Inside the niche on a grey marble pedestal stands a pyramid of red granite with a medallion bearing the profiles of the parents of Empress Maria Fyodorovna, the wife of Paul I.

This sculpture group inside the pavilion is made by one of the best Russian sculptors I. Martos.

To the east of this pavilion there is a bridge linking the Old and the New Silvia.

To the north of the bridge on the other bank of the Slavyanka there is a distinctive pavilion, a round stone tower surmounted by a conical thatch roof. It is the so-called **Pil-Tower**, built in 1797. Its name is explained by the fact that the pavilion was built on the site of a sawmill ("pilit" means "to saw" in Russian) whose machinery was driven by the waters of the Slavyanka. Pietro Gonzago skilfully painted the tower to give the impression of picturesque ruins. This, however, was just a play of fancy, a whim of the royal family. Inside the pavilion was fairly opulent. It contained a luxurious salon decorated with moulding, painting and a marble fireplace.

South of the Pil-Tower is the **Mausoleum of Paul I**, which is also often referred to as **"To My Husband and Benefactor"**. It cannot really be called a mausoleum in the true sense of the word, since the assassinated emperor was buried in the Peter and Paul Fortress and not here. As is known, in the days of old there existed the practice of putting up cenotaphs — monuments or empty tombs honouring a dead person whose body is somewhere else; the Mausoleum may be regarded as a kind of a cenotaph. This small yet majestic structure of sandstone on a granite pedestal was built in 1808-1809 to the design of Jean Thomas de Thomon in the style of an ancient Greek temple. Its main façade consists of a pediment resting on four columns made from red granite monoliths which form a semi-open pavilion. Leading to it is a broad stone staircase of nine steps. Around the walls runs a frieze of tragic masks with tears of grief. Inside the mausoleum is faced with artificial marble and illuminated through two semicircular windows in the side walls. At the back opposite the entrance there is a monument consisting of a granite pyramid with a white marble medallion bearing a portrait of Paul I. In front of the pyramid on a pedestal of porphyry there is an urn before which the figure of the emperor's widow kneels in sorrow. Next to her are the figures of his children hanging their heads in grief. This composition is the work of Ivan Martos, who, according to his contemporaries, could make even marble weep.

Photographs made in the first months after the war have preserved the tragic picture of the charred ruins to which the Pavlovsk Palace had been reduced and of the park structures destroyed by the Nazis. These documentary photographs vividly attest to the greatness of the feat performed by Soviet restorers, architects, painters and sculptors through whose selfless efforts the Pavlovsk Palace and Europe's largest park have risen renewed from the ashes.
No less selflessly did the restorers working on the other palaces and parks mentioned in this book bring their labour to the altar of universal human culture.
Praise and glory to all of them for ever and ever!

CONTENTS

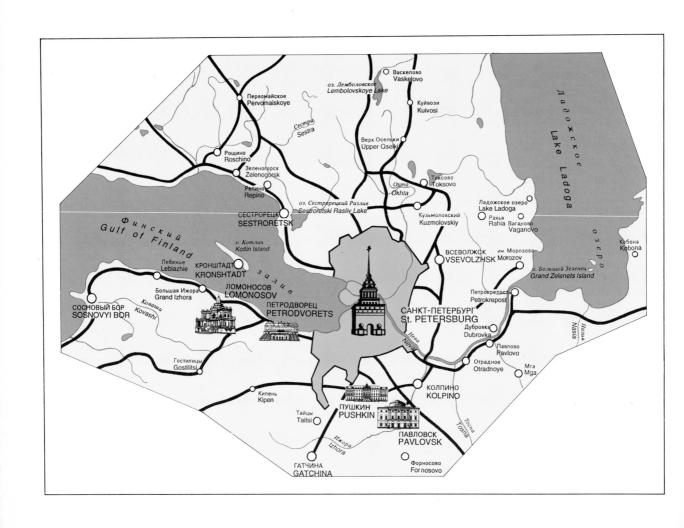